"Passionate and practical, filled with biblical insights and wisdom from lessons hard won. In *Beautiful Feet* Jessica Fick equips us to leave the footprints of our faith journey wherever we walk in life. Empowering and inspirational!"

Jo Saxton, chair of 3DMovements and author of *More Than Enchanting*

"Every woman who wants to share Jesus should read this book! Jessica uses humor, personal stories and wonderful theology not only to encourage but also to train in how to make disciples."

Greg Nettle, president, Stadia

"With a powerful and distinctly feminine voice, Fick challenges the church's understanding about the role of women in evangelistic ministry, correcting long-held assumptions about the male-dominated world of preaching evangelists. With humor, style and theological accuracy, Fick contends for the gender-inclusivity of the role of evangelist. Truly and unfortunately, a rare book celebrating the unique role women play in the work of evangelism. This book is sure to set many women free to proclaim the gospel with all the gifts and fervor the Spirit of God has given them."

R. York Moore, national evangelist, InterVarsity Christian Fellowship, author of *Making All Things New* and *Growing Your Faith by Giving It Away*

"Evangelism can be a scary journey for many of us. It's easier to say that we haven't been called to travel this road, but the truth is that God has intended for every one of us to carry and deliver the message of Jesus wherever we go. Jessica Fick understands our fears and fragilities in starting this journey. But she doesn't let us get away with avoiding the call. Instead, she challenges us with honesty, humor and heartfelt exhortations to move our beautiful feet and bring good news to a world that needs Jesus. In this much-needed book, we learn so much from Jessica and her examples in everyday witness."

Helen Lee, author of *The Missional Mom*

"I commend Jessica's book to everyone who wrongly thinks, 'people aren't interested in God.' In these chapters you'll see that God is on the move, bringing his saving story to curious and lost people through regular Christians like us."

Lon Allison, former executive director, Billy Graham Center, author of *Going Public with the Gospel*

"Evangelism isn't a calling or gifting reserved for men, and now we finally have a book that speaks directly to women with respect as those also created in God's image. Jessica Leep Fick writes with the voice of a teacher, preacher, neighbor and woman—owning and celebrating the many seasons of life, relationships, and expressions of femininity, broken and redeemed. She is a needed voice in the training up of evangelists but more importantly in our faithful, day-to-day lives as Jesus followers."

Kathy Khang, director of campus access initiatives, InterVarsity Christian Fellowship, coauthor of *More Than Serving Tea*

"Jessica's verve and sensibility combine to make *Beautiful Feet* as practical as it is inspiring. For all of us navigating the call to witness, this book is good news."

Debra Hirsch, author of *Untamed* and *Redeeming Sex*

"In her snappy, super-honest and sometimes disarmingly snarky style, Jessica Fick takes the sting out of sharing our faith. Whether we wear flip flops or stilettos, this gal challenges us all to put on shoes and walk our beautiful feet out to share our hope with our world."

Elisa Morgan, speaker, author of *The Beauty of Broken* and *Hello, Beauty Full*, cohost, *Discover the Word*

Beautiful Feet

Unleashing Women to Everyday Witness

JESSICA LEEP FICK

IVP Books

An imprint of InterVarsity Press
Downers Grove, Illinois

InterVarsity Press
P.O. Box 1400, Downers Grove, IL 60515-1426
ivpress.com
email@ivpress.com

InterVarsity Press® is the book-publishing division of InterVarsity Christian Fellowship/USA®, a movement of students and faculty active on campus at hundreds of universities, colleges and schools of nursing in the United States of America, and a member movement of the International Fellowship of Evangelical Students. For information about local and regional activities, visit intervarsity.org.

All Scripture quotations, unless otherwise indicated, are taken from THE HOLY BIBLE, NEW INTERNATIONAL VERSION®, NIV® Copyright © 1973, 1978, 1984, 2011 by Biblica, Inc.™ Used by permission. All rights reserved worldwide.

While any stories in this book are true, some names and identifying information may have been changed to protect the privacy of individuals.

Figures 7.6 and A.1 are taken from True Story *by James Choung. Copyright © 2008 by James Choung. Used by permission of InterVarsity Press, P.O. Box 1400, Downers Grove, IL 60515, USA. www.ivpress.com.*

Cover design: Cindy Kiple
Interior design: Beth McGill
Images: woman's roller skates: Jacqueline Veissid/Getty Images
    roller skates: © xavigm/iStockphoto

ISBN 978-0-8308-4320-6 (print)
ISBN 978-0-8308-9875-6 (digital)

Printed in the United States of America ∞

Library of Congress Cataloging-in-Publication Data

Fick, Jessica Leep, 1978-
Beautiful feet : unleashing women to everyday witness / Jessica Leep Fick.
    pages cm
Includes bibliographical references.
ISBN 978-0-8308-4320-6 (pbk. : alk. paper)
1. Women in missionary work. 2. Christian women--Religious life. 3. Witness bearing (Christianity) I. Title.
    BV2610.F53 2015
    248'.5082--dc23

                                                                                    2015018752

P 21 20 19 18 17 16 15 14 13 12 11 10 9 8 7 6 5 4 3 2 1

Y 32 31 30 29 28 27 26 25 24 23 22 21 20 19 18 17 16 15

To my husband, Dave—thank you for making my life

more beautiful, hilarious and thoughtful.

Contents

Can God Use Me?

The day I sensed Jesus calling me to be an evangelist, I was sitting in the back of the auditorium of a student training conference just having listened to a sermon that had nothing to do with evangelism. I had no idea how God would use me as a woman to proclaim his message. God was calling me to be an evangelist, a gospel preacher—not simply a witness.

I freaked out. Ugly-cry freaking out—the messy, heaving, snot-pouring-out, can't-catch-your-breath kind of crying. Friends whisked me outside to pray for me and comfort me because I had begun to disturb the students who were silently praying for their campuses and giving me weird looks for being so loud. Outside, sitting on a picnic table, my friends Sandy and Joe laid hands on me and tried to understand what I was saying between sobs and gulps of air. I silently prayed, *God, how is this possible? Don't you only use men as evangelists? I have no idea what this even looks like.*

Beautiful Feet

In Romans 10:14-15 Paul writes, "How, then, can they call on the one they have not believed in? And how can they believe in the one of whom they have not heard? And how can they hear without someone preaching to them? And how can anyone preach unless they are sent? As it is written: 'How beautiful are the feet of those who bring good news!'"

I couldn't see how *my* feet would be called beautiful to bring good news. I would describe them as beautiful when I had a pedicure and was wearing cute sandals. Beautiful when I was hiking through the woods of Northern Michigan with students exploring questions about God. Beautiful when I took cookies to a new neighbor whose cigarette smoke was so strong it seeped under the door of my apartment. But beautiful standing before hundreds of people, preaching the gospel and inviting people to respond to Jesus? It was terrifying and exhilarating to picture myself as a person Paul describes in the book of Romans: a preacher sent to use her beautiful feet to bring the good news to those who have never heard.

A thousand questions raced through my mind: *Should I go to seminary? How do you get training as an evangelist? Who are female role models I can look to? God, shouldn't I just stay in the background and do more relational evangelism? Isn't that what women are supposed to do? Leave the preaching up to the men? Why should I be someone who preaches? There are tons of guys who are better than me; no one is going to take me seriously. What is my husband going to think of this? People are creeped out by evangelists—that's the last way I want to describe my job.*

The tears gradually subsided as my friends prayed for me, but the questions still swirled around my mind as I sought to listen to Jesus while they prayed. As we sat on the picnic table hunched together, a cool wind blew off the bay of Lake Huron, soothing my hot and tear-stained face.

Asking Questions

I began to ask questions of Jesus and of my friends who were evangelists—mostly men who were tremendously encouraging for me to pursue this call on my life. The day after my sobbing mess of a prayer time on the picnic table, my friend Mark took a walk with me and listened to all my questions. We walked down the curving camp road of InterVarsity's Cedar Campus, past the cozy cabins, the groves of fragrant cedar trees and the wooden sign marking the Narnia trail. My biggest question was how to develop as an evangelist. If Jesus was calling me to this, I wanted to take it seriously and grow in whatever ways possible. "You will be on the frontlines of ministry, Jessica," Mark shared as we walked down the winding camp road. "I heard Ravi Zacharias, the famed evangelist, once say something to the effect that evangelists should have more training than pastors because they are preaching and relating to people far from God and need to know their stuff about Scripture better than anyone."

I mulled this over. The thought of taking languages and spending years debating theology with mostly white dudes in a seminary was completely unappealing to me; it felt like a waste of my time and money and didn't seem essential for me to fulfill this new calling. What Mark said made sense—I would need to study, I would need to know *why* Jesus is the Way, the Truth and the Life and be able to explain it and preach it in a compelling and accessible way to people who don't believe. That was exciting. That was challenging. That made me eager to go to those people who had questions, doubts and fears and tell them the good news about Jesus.

After that week I still had a lot of questions, fears and confusion. I certainly didn't look like most of the people I knew who had been called to make important decisions for the church about how to reach people with the gospel. When I showed up to present my missionary report about our campus ministry, I felt like I either had to blend in or suppress who I was around the white-haired Dutch men in their suits who made important decisions for the churches they served in Grand Rapids, Michigan. I felt marginalized, mini-mized and stigmatized—like an adult who is relegated to sit at the kids' table at a family gathering.

Even my own pastor, when I met with him for pancakes to share about God's call on my life, seemed suspicious. Pastors and teachers fit into the rubric of what normal ministers are—evangelists and prophets don't. Evangelists and prophets are unpredictable and make people feel uncomfortable. Yet they are essential to the mission of God. Even more confused after I left the Real Food café, I felt like I had three strikes against me: one, that I was a woman; two, that I was now identifying myself as an evangelist; and three, that I didn't want to take the traditional seminary route to become more educated. It felt a little like the Orthodox Jewish prayer: "Thank you God for not making me a slave, a gentile or a woman." They may not have been the same strikes that kept me from ministering, but there were certainly unspoken restrictions and attitudes that dis-couraged me from pursuing a call as an evangelist.

Who Are My Role Models?

At the core of my doubts was the need to answer the question, Can God use me, just as I am as a woman, to proclaim his good news? I struggled to see how Paul's words in Romans 10 applied to me, and sometimes I still do. I could picture Billy Graham. But I wasn't a white, southern man with a booming voice like a lion. I could think of Beth Moore or other women speakers—speakers but not specifically evangelists. My vision was dissonant with the picture I had of most women speakers. It seemed women speakers got lumped in with two different types of ministries: disempow-ering "pink devotional, let's serve coffee after church and be really nice and learn a ton about the Bible" types of women preachers, or

> Can God use me, just as I am as a woman, to proclaim his good news?

militant "feminist" women preachers who were always talking about the need for a more egalitarian church and wore hemp clothing and ate a lot of lentils. Both images left me with wanting something more and believing that Jesus' mission was bigger than being nice or fighting about gender issues. I could name only one woman evangelist at the time: Becky Pippert. Becky had also been a campus minister with my movement, InterVarsity Christian Fellowship, and had written *Out of the Saltshaker*, which *Christianity Today* named one of the top fifty books to have influenced evangelicals.

Three years after my messy crying realization I was preparing to go to the Urbana Student Missions Conference. In reviewing the list of seminars I saw that Becky Pippert was leading one, so I tracked her down and asked her to have breakfast with me. Fortunately she wasn't weirded out by my eagerness. She graciously sat with me, eating eggs and toast while I peppered her with questions. Becky was more than happy to pray for me, share her experiences and help me think through how to pursue my call to preach the good news. It was a defining moment—to sit with the only woman I knew of who was living out the call to be an evangelist.

I left our breakfast grateful and encouraged, a little starstruck, and longing to see more women like Becky—an army of women who boldly and lovingly share Jesus. Women who help to train up the next generation of evangelists and who are willing to proclaim Jesus wherever they go.

Can God Use You?

God wants to use your beautiful feet, but are they willing to go? Like me, you might have doubts, fears and insecurities swirling around your mind. And it's likely that they've immobilized you with overbearing guilt that you aren't sharing Jesus, or gotten you caught up in comparing yourself to other people who fit an ideal of what it means to be a faithful witness. But Paul's words in

Romans apply to you too: "How beautiful are your feet that bring good news!" What holds you back from believing that God calls your feet beautiful too?

> What holds you back from believing that God calls your feet beautiful too?

As you read this book, invite the Holy Spirit to give you a clearer picture of who you are—warts, beauty, eccentricities and all. I hope you'll feel a sense of solidarity with other women who have been using their beautiful feet for thousands of years to bring the good news of Jesus, and that you'll see yourself in the stories. Laugh, cry, reflect and talk with girlfriends about what motivates you to share Jesus and what holds you back. I've provided a discussion guide at the back of the book for you to think through what it will mean for you to be unleashed into everyday witness. Bake some brownies, grab a drink and curl up on each other's couches to talk about how you can use your beautiful feet to share the good news on your campuses and in your communities and workplaces.

I hope that the resources provided will help you to take baby steps and giant leaps forward in sharing the love of Jesus. I'm praying that the Holy Spirit will walk with you as you pause to explore your internal world and move forward to respond, loving people in practical ways. And I hope that you will feel great joy, purpose and excitement as you follow Jesus in his mission to love those who are far from him. It doesn't really matter what your feet look like, how you feel about them, what other people have said about them or what you wish they could do.

You. Have. Beautiful. Feet. So let's use them together.

Uncomfortable

It's difficult for a fish to describe the water it swims in. Even if it is murky and polluted, that water is all the fish has ever known. I used to feel this way in some of my Christian environments. There was something off about the way men and women related, but it was difficult to describe what that was since it seemed to be a normal part of the culture. Growing up I saw women serve as pastors, elders and deacons. The Christian Reformed church my husband and I attended in Grand Rapids made a point to include women and people of color in leadership positions. However, in my work as a campus missionary, I was required to raise support with many different types of individuals and churches—many that held very different views on women in ministry inside and outside of their churches. I can remember sitting in an air-conditioned sanctuary during an elder board meeting of a more conservative church that didn't include women on their governing boards or in their pulpits. I was waiting to give a testimony about how God had been moving on campus through the ministry I work for, InterVarsity Christian Fellowship, and to thank them for the grant that they had given me to do this work. I sat there in the hard oak pew wearing black dress pants and a nice blue shirt, conscious that I was the only woman—and the youngest person—in the room.

At one point a mom interrupted the meeting with a baby on her hip, towing a toddler behind her. Under her arm was a folder that she was bringing to her husband, who had forgotten it at home. She looked bedraggled, tired and a sharp contrast to the suited churchmen all around her. The moderator thanked her, and all the men in the room looked at her as she left, children beginning to scream on their way back out to the car on a hot June day.

I don't know what was going through the minds of the men that day. But as I considered the contrast of these church elders making important decisions in their suits and the frazzled mom with the two kids, I assumed they were looking at her with pity. These men might have been feeling tenderhearted toward this mom and her kids, but in *my* mind, I silently made a vow to myself: *I will never be seen like that. She is seen as just a woman. Just a mom. Just a deliverer of important documents. Not included in the important decisions. She is not welcome here. She doesn't fit.* It was a vow of resignation rather than anger, resentment or sadness over what it was like to be viewed as a woman in this context.

Little did I know that I would one day become like the frazzled mom in the church that day with my own kids *and* be one helping to make important decisions for her church. But that day the reality of the world around me was that I was an anomaly in the church and the frazzled mom was the norm. I wanted to be seen as powerful, important enough to be included at the table of decision, worthy enough to have my voice heard inside and outside of the church. In short, I wanted to be a man.

Now before you think I started researching sex-change surgery, let me explain how most people would see me on a given day. I love sparkly things. Turning me loose in a jewelry store like Charming Charlie is like putting a salt lick in front of a deer.[1] No one could mistake me for being a man with my Marilyn Monroe–esque curves. I love being married to my husband and doing all the things that God intended to happen in a healthy marriage. I love fashion and come from a family of women who have modeled, sold makeup, acted on stage and owned multiple fur coats. My mom took me to the Clinique counter when I was a tween to buy me a makeup starter kit because she said, "I'm not going to let you ruin your skin with that cheap wet n wild stuff." I was doomed to the high-end makeup counter for the rest of my life, even while scraping by as a missionary raising support.

Yet as I sat in the church that day, I was despising this woman not because she was doing anything wrong, but because I despised myself as a woman. I hated that God seemed to create me to lack the power, influence, physical height and loud voice of a man. There were insecurities I needed to work through, as well as shame and self-contempt from which I needed healing to believe God had created me how he intended me. I needed healing personally, but also missionally. Even if my church or Christian culture around me didn't value how God had created me, I needed to believe that God sent me with my beautiful feet to preach good news.

I began to realize that I could never fully engage in the mission God had given me if I hated who he had created me to be. I was comfortable on a dance floor, leading a meeting, telling stories to friends and making them laugh. I didn't give a second thought to what I said, how I moved or what I wore. I liked who I was in those contexts. But stepping out to preach the gospel seemed to stir up a lie I had believed: *You don't belong here. You aren't enough. People will look down on you. You will never fit because you are a woman.* As a woman trying to figure out her calling, the experience of preaching

> Even if my church or Christian culture around me didn't value how God had created me, I needed to believe that God sent me with my beautiful feet to preach good news.

didn't feel as comfortable for me to step into. I waded through
whether I was simply insecure, or if there were systems, structures
and attitudes at play that made it difficult for me to pursue God's
call on my life.

Gender and the Body of Christ

In *Christianity Today*'s article "The Seminary Gender Gap," Sharon
Hodde Miller asks why seminaries continue to be predominantly
male, reinforcing the impression that men are preferable for ministry leadership than women.

> [Several] factors produce a persistent minority of female,
> evangelical seminarians with a rather tumultuous seminary
> experience. Evangelical women who discern a call to sem-
> inary often find themselves without much community and
> without many resources. Whether or not they are seeking
> ordination, women report feeling ostracized by male class-
> mates. Among the evangelical women I have interviewed,
> most experienced little interaction with the men in their
> classes, and were even treated as a sexual temptation.[2]

At evangelical seminaries women make up one in five of the students pursuing an MDiv.[3] When systems, structures and people
within the church and seminaries communicate the message that
women don't belong, are objects of sexual temptation to be feared
and will receive little to no help during their seminary experience
with few job prospects after graduation, it is no wonder that so many
of us hate ourselves and resent God for making us women. When
the internal fears of whether you are enough are only reinforced by
the culture around you, what other options are there for believing
anything else?

As God has healed me of my misogyny and helped me navigate
around this painful reality in the church, I see my friends who believe

they are exempt from leadership and witness because of their gender. Women who have the power of Jesus to change the world believe their life can only be Pinteresting, not missional, because they're a wife or a mom. I pray with female students who tell me that they feel worthless because God made them a woman. I hear the stories of women preachers who are sent emails about the clothes they wear to preach on Sunday mornings while their male counterparts receive none of these types of emails. I attend Christian leadership conferences with men as presenters and see the only woman on stage giggle when her husband tells the crowd of thousands how much he wants to go and have sex with his wife. The crowd laughs, but I sit and wonder, *Is this all? Are women just seen here as objects for personal pleasure and procreation? Am I seen like that as one of the few women at this conference because I wear high heels and jewelry?*

I hear all of these things and I see all of these broken realities and I feel dismayed. Yet it makes me long for Jesus to make something new—in my own life and in the

> Are women just seen here as objects for personal pleasure and procreation? Am I seen like that . . . because I wear high heels and jewelry?

church. I long for Jesus to heal the hurting female college students I serve and the bored and frustrated women in the church who want to lead, and I long for the dudes who don't even realize any of this is happening to become aware and repent. I want to see a whole, healthy church with women and men leading and loving Jesus in all that he has created his church to be. Carolyn Custis James, in her book *Half the Church*, writes of a vision of men and women working together as God's sons and daughters. She refers to this force as the Blessed Alliance. She writes, "The Blessed Alliance is central to God's kingdom strategy for the world. Without it we are pursuing kingdom work at a serious disadvantage."[4]

In prayer, God continues to lead me back to his life-giving

Scriptures. There in his living Word he tells me who I am, who he

> I want to see a whole, healthy church with women and men leading and loving Jesus in all that he has created his church to be.

is and what he thinks about me as a woman. And it's good stuff. Recently I read 1 Corinthians 12, and in the context of all the thoughts, fears and pain swirling around my heart, Jesus led me to these words:

> Just as a body, though one, has many parts, but all its many parts form one body, so it is with Christ. For we were all baptized by one Spirit so as to form one body—whether Jews or Gentiles, slave or free—and we were all given the one Spirit to drink. Even so the body is not made up of one part but of many.
>
> Now if the foot should say, "Because I am not a hand, I do not belong to the body," it would not for that reason stop being part of the body. And if the ear should say, "Because I am not an eye, I do not belong to the body," it would not for that reason stop being part of the body. If the whole body were an eye, where would the sense of hearing be? If the whole body were an ear, where would the sense of smell be? *But in fact God has placed the parts in the body, every one of them, just as he wanted them to be.* If they were all one part, where would the body be? As it is, there are many parts, but one body. . . .
>
> There should be no division in the body, but . . . *its parts should have equal concern for each other. If one part suffers, every part suffers with it; if one part is honored, every part rejoices with it.* (1 Corinthians 12:12-20, 25-26)

I want to draw your attention to the verses put in italics. This passage talks about the unity and diversity of the body of Christ, beginning with what would happen in the body if each part wanted to be something different or to just leave the body. The first italicized verse says, "But in fact God has placed the parts in the body, every one of them, just as he wanted them to be." Reading this verse it was as if Jesus said to me, "Jessica, I have placed you exactly where I want you to be. *It is not a mistake that you are a woman.* You aren't a loser. I have placed you just as I want you to be right here and right now." I began to feel a calm come over my heart and growing gratitude for Jesus' unchanging, unbreakable love for me regardless of how I looked, felt or thought of myself; regardless of what people said or thought about me; regardless of whether I was included or excluded.

Yet I continued to pray and question: *But Jesus, what about all the dudes who can zoom ahead in their careers because though they might have young children they aren't the ones breastfeeding the baby? Why am I not getting the same opportunities? What about the fact that women have actually been described throughout history as "the weaker sex"? This is not cool.*[5] He answered me in his Word: "[The body's] parts should have equal concern for each other. If one part suffers, every part suffers with it; if one part is honored, every part rejoices with it." The Lord seemed to speak from the page: "My church is suffering because my daughters are suffering." I couldn't get the faces of friends, students and moms out of my mind who had silently suffered wounds inside and outside of the church because of their gender. I thought about the 603 million women across the world who live in fear of abuse because domestic abuse is not outlawed and rape within marriage is not considered a crime.[6] I thought of the many women who believe that their gifts, abilities and passions are dispensable in their churches or ministries. My own painful experiences came to mind—times when I was accused of not submitting to my husband because I preached; when I was told that I was foolish to go to graduate school because I had a baby; or when I shared about my work of traveling and preaching and women asked, "I could never do that, how can you do that? Wow, that must be rough." (I never knew how to answer that question other than, "Jesus. Jesus is how I can do this.")

Jesus continued to speak. "Let my daughters know they have beautiful feet. Let them know they are sent, called, restored and indispensable to me and to my kingdom. Let my daughters know I have created them just as I want them to be. I don't make mistakes. I see their suffering. And in the midst of suffering I am making something new in their lives and in the church."

Let's Dance

What would happen if we didn't have feet? Picture that. Picture legs with stumps at the end. People couldn't even use crutches to get around because you need at least one foot to help you balance as you move. Feet help us to be balanced and agile, to grip, to move, to protect. Some feet have warts, calluses, scars, chipped toenail paint or malformations. Some have blisters or are covered up with socks. Others are dirty and without shoes. There is no qualifier on what makes feet beautiful according to the verse in Romans. Your feet *are* beautiful. Not because of how they look but because they are an essential part of how God demonstrates his love for the world. Feet aren't designed just to be admired. They are designed to help us move, go places and respond in love to the needs around us. God has given you beautiful feet for a purpose. And you get to use them uniquely in how he is directing you to share his good news.

I want you to see more of what God has for you. I hope that as you read you'll begin to see that Jesus loves you and has created you uniquely and perfectly to bring good news to others. I want you to walk with Jesus into the broken places in your life where you've believed the lie that you aren't enough and, with him guiding you through those dark places, begin to step into the woman Jesus has made you to be.

As the Holy Spirit bolsters your confidence that you actually do have beautiful feet that can bring good news, I want to give you some practical ways to share his good news. I hope that you won't just enjoy the healing or insight that come as God meets you, but that you'll tell others about the good things Jesus is doing in your life. We get to do this as a community—we get to use our beautiful feet together to bring his good news into the world.

Jesus wants us to speak and live out his gospel. And his Holy Spirit is able to guide us in exactly how to do so. When we aren't attuned to the voice of the Holy Spirit we miss out on the life Jesus has for us. We miss out on the adventure of witness. We only faintly grasp the transforming power of the gospel in our lives and the lives of others. It is as if we are choosing to deafen ourselves to the bigger-than-Dolby-digital, high-fidelity, stereo-surround life God intended us to live. It's like we're milling around in the hallway of God's great dance party, tapping our feet to the bass thump when Jesus has been saying, "What the heck are you doing out here?! Come in! You are invited! Dance! Move! Have fun! Get down wit' yo bad self!"

Sisters, you are too important to God and his mission to keep silent and be still. You are indispensable. I am praying that as the Holy Spirit speaks to you through Scriptures, stories of other women and my experiences, you will be empowered to share Jesus wherever he has sent you. I am praying for healing, protection and power that can only come from Jesus for the church and his people as we navigate through what it means to honor every part of the body. You have beautiful feet—and the Holy Spirit is inviting you to follow him in the adventure of sharing Jesus.

Response

What are three things you like about how God has created you? It could be anything from having a natural compassion toward people to having strong legs that help you do long distance runs. What are lies you've believed about yourself that have hindered you in life and witness?

We Saw Your Boobs

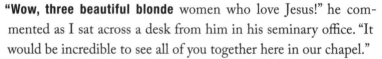

"Wow, three beautiful blonde women who love Jesus!" he commented as I sat across a desk from him in his seminary office. "It would be incredible to see all of you together here in our chapel."

I had begun exploring seminary as a way to live out my call to be an evangelist and had scheduled a slew of visits to seminaries around West Michigan. During this particular visit I mentioned other female students I knew who attended their program and how much they'd enjoyed working on their Masters of Divinity degrees. I felt uncomfortable that he chose to point out that the three of us were "beautiful blonde women," not because it was untrue, but because he seemed more concerned with our appearance than our ministry giftedness or calling. I was exploring a ministry degree, not interviewing for a Christian beauty pageant. Needless to say, I decided not to go to seminary at this institution.

Rachel Pietka wrote an article called "Hey John Piper, Is My Femininity Showing?"[1] that echoes the sadness and frustrations I've felt for years about how women are often viewed in the church. The article focuses on how John Piper, as a complementarian pastor, simultaneously rejects and obsesses over women's bodies when women preach or speak publically. I don't know what John Piper's past is like, what he struggles with or what his relationships with women are like. I admire that he was vulnerable and self-aware enough to admit that he at times struggles in his interactions with women to know how to appropriately relate to and think about them. It's important to be aware of situations or people where temptations arise. However, precautions are so often taken to extreme measures, giving women the impression that there is something wrong with them and that it is their fault that men sin.

Ann Boyd shared on the blog *The Well* that when she was in college she and the other members of her campus group were trying to figure out how to live a God-honoring life. Naturally this extended to the area of sexuality.

> One group of excellent young men got together regularly to discuss strategies in their pursuit of holiness. They encouraged each other to live lives of purity, and they took seriously Paul's admonition to "flee from sin." Unfortunately, this turned sour as they began to practice "fleeing" from women. If they came into the presence of a woman whom they found attractive in some way, they would shout "flee!" and start running the other direction. Looking back, this is a bit comical, and could be very funny on film. But in real life, as a woman in her early twenties trying to figure out how to live, this was not helpful to me. The women in our community were all quite conservative in our dress and actions, but it seemed that just the fact that we were women with, God help us, female bodies, defined us as objects of temptation.[2]

The problem is, when prominent pastors, teachers or theologians begin to affirm that men can't listen to women without falling into temptation to lust over them, it sends the message that women's bodies are inherently evil, something to cover up and be ashamed of. It teaches men that women are objects of temptation to be leery of, especially when doing something as holy as teaching Scripture. It teaches women to be ashamed of their bodies and that something is intrinsically wrong with them as embodied beings. When we approach being embodied from this perspective, we shift the focus from the problem of the sin that exists inside each of us to our need to control the things that tempt us. Jesus taught in Mark 7:15, "It's not what goes into your body that defiles you; you are defiled by what comes from your heart" (NLT). He goes on to say, "It is what comes from inside that defiles you. For from within, out of a person's heart, come evil thoughts, sexual immorality, theft, murder, adultery, greed, wickedness, deceit, lustful desires, envy, slander, pride, and foolishness. All these vile things come from within; they are what defile you" (Mark 7:20-23 NLT).

We are afraid of the evil that lurks in each of us, so we often make awkward rules and strategies—like yelling "flee!" when talking with an attractive woman—to try and deal with what is bubbling up in our own hearts. I was getting ready to preach once and had on a then-trendy poncho. The pastor, who had been helping me develop as a preacher at that time, asked, "Did you choose that outfit to cover your womanly figure?" I was caught off guard by the pointed question. Unfortunately, I didn't ask him what prompted his question about my poncho. I assumed that he was concerned about me tempting people because I happen to be a preacher with boobs.

In the Pulpit, in the Pew, What's a Gal Supposed to Do?

So what do we do when we are called to be witnesses to the ends of the earth but we get stopped short because we have boobs? Or we stop before we even begin to witness because we feel self-conscious that we have boobs? Or we have been mistreated or verbally or physically assaulted because we have boobs, or curvy hips or a Beyonce-esque booty? Or we have been told all our lives that we are second-class citizens because we are women? The conversation about the role of women in the church isn't simply about who is staying most true to Scripture and theology about gender. Women are wondering, *Is my body a liability or an asset in the work God is calling me to? Is there something wrong with me because I'm a woman?* Lurking behind those vehement conversations and arguments is the unspoken question: "How do men and women relate to one another as embodied beings? How do we honor the people God has made us to be?" The conversation needs to move beyond legalistic rules and outward objectification. It isn't just female speakers who deal with this issue of being embodied and proclaiming the gospel. It's every woman who is seeking to share Jesus. And it will continue to affect the mission of the church unless the Holy Spirit moves in power to bring deep healing to the ways men and women see themselves and each other.

This raises all kinds of questions and likely some painful memories about ways that you have been excluded or marginalized or felt self-conscious because Jesus chose to make you a woman. That's right. He *chose* you. Being formed as a baby girl in the womb wasn't God's consolation prize. He created you just as you are, from the color of your hair and skin to the ways your fingernails have ridges. You are a chosen, sent one of God just the way you are. Nothing more. Nothing less. And God wants you to utilize all that he has given you to proclaim his glory and salvation to others. Yes, even boobs can proclaim the glory of God (and not just to teenage boys).

Convert or Flirt?

A few years ago my husband and I co-led a trip to Kingston, Jamaica, for InterVarsity students from the United States to partner in an evangelistic outreach with Jamaican students on their campus. We visited several campuses across the island and set up interactive art and evangelism booths called Proxē Stations, a tool two of my brilliant colleagues Beth and Dave created.

Aubrey, a blonde, blue-eyed hipster from Michigan, was boldly sharing Jesus at one of the Proxē Stations. She was explaining the gospel as she talked about what it means for God to give us a heart makeover. She talked with male and female students, and I was so proud of her for trusting Jesus to use her as his messenger. Standing in that dirt parking lot where the student activities fair was set up, I saw her bow her head and pray with two highschool students. I was elated thinking that they were perhaps inviting Jesus to be the Lord of their lives.

As we were packing up for the day, I walked over to Aubrey. The sounds of techno bass thumps filled the air as another group set up stacks of speakers for a dubstep party. Though I had seen Aubrey faithfully and boldly sharing Jesus all day, she looked discouraged and uncomfortable.

"So tell me about those girls you prayed with," I said excitedly. "What did you talk about with them?"

Aubrey shared how the girls had struggled with depression and that, out of her own testimony of meeting God in the midst of depression, she invited the girls to invite Jesus to heal them and lead their lives.

"That's great! Praise God!" I exclaimed.

"Yeah!" she said, though her enthusiasm was half-hearted.

Aubrey glanced around to see if other students were listening to our conversation.

"There was this guy at the end of the day," Aubrey said. "He seemed really interested in the gospel. I shared it with him and we had a really good conversation about some of his family struggles. At the end of the conversation, when I was taking down his contact information so students could follow up with him, he hit on me and asked for my phone number because he thought I was sexy and wanted to stay in touch." Aubrey looked down at the dusty ground, ashamed as if she had done something wrong.

"So what did you do?" I asked, scenes flashing through my mind of similar experiences I'd had.

"I was so flustered that I just told him that I wasn't interested and that one of the Jamaican students would be happy to talk with him about what it means to follow Jesus."

She looked at me with sadness and confusion. "Is this always going to happen? If I talk to guys about Jesus, are they just going to hit on me? How do I know if they're actually interested in Jesus and not just flirting with me?"

I sighed and said, "Look. We cannot control how people will respond to us. You are beautiful, and it's going to be hard for anyone not to notice that."

She smiled a little, slightly uncomfortable at my compliment.

"Jesus is more beautiful than any of us could hope to be," I went on. "Though people may initially be attracted to how you look, your personality or style, Jesus is the one who can open their hearts to see what they are really longing for: a relationship with him. You can't help who God made you to be. And you shouldn't hide it either. Ultimately, you will need to choose if how people respond to you is going to keep you from sharing Jesus, or if you'll trust him even when 'distractions'—like how hot you are—are what initially attract people to talk to you. Jesus gave you this body, this face, and he wants to use it all for his glory and to draw people to himself."

The experience with Aubrey has stuck in my mind and made me wonder how many other women experience this dynamic. And how many other women simply stop sharing their faith because of awkward experiences like this.

Embodied

My conversation with Aubrey wasn't an encouragement to use her

womanly wiles to attract dudes to Jesus. It was simply an acknowl-
edgment that people will likely want to talk with her because she's
beautiful, in addition to being intelligent, funny and kind. Because
how she looks is the first impression people will have of her, why
would it not be something Jesus could use to draw others to
himself? Even with that being said, women need to be careful because guys *do* get the wrong impression at times.

There aren't many helpful ways for men and women to talk
about being embodied without it getting weird. And because
it's weird, we don't address it other than to say that God loves
us for more than our appearance. But what do we do with the
fact that he has made us embodied with feet, eyes, mouths, hips
and hair? With a specific skin tone, cultural background and
interests? My friend Stephanie, a spunky Taiwanese American
campus minister, shared her frustrating story of witness with
me that underscores the challenge of embodiment for women
sharing their faith.

> I've been reaching out intentionally to a community in my
> martial arts class for the last half year, where I've made it clear
> that I love Jesus, attend church regularly, pray, live out my
> faith, etc. I have fun with this community and have really
> grown to love them. However, one of the community
> members has strong "yellow fever."[3] This is one of the places
> where I believe my witness is hindered by how I look. I love
> being Taiwanese American and I love being a female. But in
> this case, I feel hindered with this guy—I feel objectified and
> extremely uncomfortable around him. It's also been difficult
> to invite him to meet my Christian community (of mostly
> Asians) because when I have, every time I turn around he's
> talking to another Asian girl! I know he's hurting and that
> Jesus wants to care for him, but I don't want to give off signals

of intimacy. He's even asked to go to church with me (an evangelist's dream!). I would have said yes . . . except that he asked if he could sleep at my apartment the night before . . . where I live with two other Asian women. UM. NO. What is a girl to do? I just want him to know Jesus! I have compassion for the guy but I'm also disgusted.

Embodiment is a perpetual challenge for women preachers and speakers. As we step into the pulpit, there are always lingering questions in the back of our minds: Will I be seen as nothing more than my body? My ethnicity? My hairstyle? The clothing I chose to wear? As I deliver the Word of God that I've prayed over, studied and worked hard to prepare, will the people listening reduce me to what I'm wearing or how God has shaped my body?

A female pastor (who chose to remain anonymous) wrote a piece for *Christianity Today* about how she decides what to wear to preach on Sunday mornings.

As a professional communicator, I put a lot of thought into what I'm going to say and how I'm going to say it. Surely the amount of thought I give to how I dress should be insignificant? But clothing is also a form of communication. Whether I like it or not, people make assessments about me and my message and my church based on how I look. If I employ tone of voice, multi-media, body language to communicate my message, why not use everything at my disposal, including my appearance, to support the goals I'm trying to accomplish here? *All things to all people and all that. . . .*

While ministry is not about me, I believe that God ministers through my life and experience. *Yes! It's okay for me to have a personality and express it.* Look at Dan Kimball's pompadour, Shane Claiborne's do-rag, Rick Warren's Hawaiian shirts, Alan Hirsch's goatee. They bring who they are into their teaching and leadership. It makes them seem more human. It makes their stories of God more real.[4]

You get the picture. A woman preacher has to think through all of these questions because she is embodied. God has chosen to carry his message through her—someone who went through puberty, grew boobs, began menstruating and became a woman. It all feels a little too earthy, doesn't it? Almost as gross as a baby being born among the foul smell of animal manure to a mother who bled onto the hay as she contracted and pushed out the Son of God into the world. Embodied. This is exactly what God intended when he sent Jesus into the world—that he would take a physical form, and that people could see the sunlight on his tired face, throw their arms around his shoulders to hug him and follow his path down dusty roads. It's uncomfortable to think about being embodied because it just doesn't seem very spiritual.

Sexual Healing

Without some major healing within the church—let alone outside it—I doubt others will come to the conclusion that I eventually have: God gave women their bodies. And he called them good. We need to understand how broken our view of one another has become because of sin. We need to repent and begin to see that God thought about boobs too. He saw them when he formed me, just like he saw my hazel eyes, my genes that are predisposed to diabetes and, oddly enough, like my brother Matt, my three extra wisdom teeth.

> Without some major healing within the church—let alone outside it—I doubt others will come to the conclusion that I eventually have: God gave women their bodies. And he called them good.

I've had men ogle me because of what I chose to wear when I preached. I've had men refuse to look at me when I preach. I've had men and women make comments about what is modest/fashionable/permissible to wear when I preach. And you know what I've concluded? God was pleased because he made me in his image and has the right view of men and women: he sees us as his beloved children and as partners in a blessed alliance to bring his message to the ends of the earth. Not only did he see my boobs, but God also saw my brain that constantly dreams up crazy ideas of how to reach more people with the gospel. He saw my love of color, art and form, and my delight at creating an aesthetically pleasing outfit to wear when I'm at the playground with my children or when I'm preaching before thousands of people.

Perhaps more than making rules about what people should and shouldn't wear and how we interact with each other as embodied people, we should repent and ask the Holy Spirit to heal us of our brokenness and sin. We need to extend grace, offer forgiveness and practice long-suffering with each other as we figure out how to love each other as Christ intended.

Men, Women and Jesus

Jesus shows us a different way of relating to one another as men and women and seeing ourselves as embodied people. In John 4, Jesus talks with the Samaritan woman at the well. Brenda Salter McNeil affectionately calls her "Sam," since she isn't named in the text.[5]

> Jesus shows us a different way of relating to one another as men and women and seeing ourselves as embodied people.

> So he came to a town in Samaria called Sychar, near the plot of ground Jacob had given to his son Joseph. Jacob's well was there, and Jesus, tired as he was from the journey, sat down by the well. It was about noon.
>
> When a Samaritan woman came to draw water, Jesus said

to her, "Will you give me a drink?" (His disciples had gone into the town to buy food.)

The Samaritan woman said to him, "You are a Jew and I am a Samaritan woman. How can you ask me for a drink?" (For Jews do not associate with Samaritans.)

Jesus answered her, "If you knew the gift of God and who it is that asks you for a drink, you would have asked him and he would have given you living water."

"Sir," the woman said, "you have nothing to draw with and the well is deep. Where can you get this living water? Are you greater than our father Jacob, who gave us the well and drank from it himself, as did also his sons and his livestock?"

Jesus answered, "Everyone who drinks this water will be thirsty again, but whoever drinks the water I give them will never thirst. Indeed, the water I give them will become in them a spring of water welling up to eternal life."

The woman said to him, "Sir, give me this water so that I won't get thirsty and have to keep coming here to draw water."

He told her, "Go, call your husband and come back."

"I have no husband," she replied.

Jesus said to her, "You are right when you say you have no husband. The fact is, you have had five husbands, and the man you now have is not your husband. What you have just said is quite true." (John 4:5-18)

Jesus sent his disciples away for food so he could talk to the woman. The two of them were alone, and she was a woman of shady character. How would this look to other people? Currently there are some men and pastors who won't meet with women in a public place or drive in a car together for fear of people seeing them together and assuming that something inappropriate is happening. The fear of scandal, the possibility of impurity and the judgments of others hinder witness to women and reinforce the belief that there is something inherently wrong with them. This is why we need the Holy Spirit to guide us and to help us deal with our own fears and others' skepticism when witness begins to cross gender barriers. Through the Spirit we can trust that Jesus will convict us and turn our hearts to love our brothers and sisters, to care more about demonstrating the love of Christ to lonely and marginalized women than fearing that our reputation will be ruined.

> Just then his disciples returned and were surprised to find him talking with a woman. But no one asked, "What do you want?" or "Why are you talking with her?"
>
> Then, leaving her water jar, the woman went back to the town and said to the people, "Come, see a man who told me everything I ever did. Could this be the Messiah?" They came out of the town and made their way toward him. . . .
>
> They said to the woman, "We no longer believe just because of what you said; now we have heard for ourselves, and we know that this man really is the Savior of the world." (John 4:27-30, 42)

Jesus saw "Sam" as one loved by God but marred by her own sin and the sins of others. He related to her as a friend, a brother and the Messiah who was the only one who could save her. What is significant in this passage is the way Jesus mobilized her to be a witness. The Samaritan woman moved from encountering Jesus to becoming an evangelist to all of her neighbors. Her whole town responded, perhaps because they were amazed to see the transformation this woman experienced.

What would have happened that day if Jesus hadn't talked to the woman because she was alone? Because she was beautiful? Because she had a reputation? Because others thought poorly of her? We see the disciples' obvious discomfort when they return to find Jesus talking with the Samaritan woman. It's as if a record scratched at a party when the nerd said something awkward and all the cool kids stopped dancing and stared at him. You can feel the question hanging in the air that the disciples wanted to ask but didn't: "Jesus, what are you doing with *her?*" I can picture it being so uncomfortable for the woman to have the disciples stare—and maybe even glare—at her, that she left. And she told her town about the man who told her everything she had ever done. The same people who ignored her, perhaps looked away when she walked down the street, whispered about her or ogled her lovely body are the ones who tell her that they believe that Jesus is the Savior of the world because of what she has told them.

If she had not dropped her water jar and used her beautiful feet to go into town to tell others about Jesus, the whole town would have missed out. In this interaction, Jesus profoundly demonstrated a new way of how men and women could relate to one another. We find healing in and through him and are able to go back to our homes and towns to share how he has healed and forgiven us from all the ways we have been hurt and hurt one another. Jesus is able to move us out of feeling self-conscious or marginalized because of how others view us. Jesus is able to move us from an encounter with him to evangelism to many.

> Jesus profoundly demonstrated a new way of how men and women could relate to one another.

Call Me

I took some female evangelists I was mentoring to a dive bar in Cleveland to do some karaoke and conversational evangelism. We sat down at the bar to order drinks and were well aware of the attention we were drawing. Helping my mentees think through their own embodied voice, I had asked them to choose three words that described themselves, to ask five friends to describe them and then to pick a song that embodied those traits. Being a good leader, I offered to do karaoke first. I was nervous—I'm not a very good singer, and I felt the pressure of modeling crosscultural leadership to my mentees. Billy Wayne, the karaoke master, popped in the CD with Blondie's "Call Me"—my song of choice—and I tried to channel my inner Debbie Harry. It was pretty pathetic, but I lived it up the best I could and danced and sang to try and entertain and connect with the few people in the bar. Afterward I was walking back to my seat when an obese man playing pool motioned to me and said, "I'll call you! What's your number?"

I have had to deal with situations like this enough that it's given me a chance to pause and reflect. How can I embody Christ's love in this situation where I am being approached because I'm a lovely lady? People go to bars because they want to connect with someone and are looking for community. My three mentees stared at me, wondering what I was going to do. Would I be offended that he would hit on me? Chastise him and tell him he was being gross? Ignore him? I decided to high-five him, laugh and say, "Yeah, my number is 555-1212—call me anytime!" (This was a kind yet clear way to say "I'm not interested" while still responding to this person who is also made in the image of God.)[6] We both started laughing, knowing that I had given him the number for information. He went back to playing pool and I sat down with my girls.

That night we were able to share with the people around us that we were campus missionaries hoping to grow in our confidence in who God made us to be. This intrigued every person we shared with, and it drew them to talk with us and offer to buy us drinks rather than assume we were going to shut them down if they tried to strike up a conversation. Hopefully we left them with the fragrance of Christ. Based on the positive ways people responded to us when we told them we were missionaries for Jesus, I think they got a good whiff of his love for them that night.

Use Your God-Given Assets

In *More Than Serving Tea*, Nikki Toyama writes,

> Evangelism was so hard for me. I didn't identify with the
> people who stand on street corners and debate. I didn't feel
> comfortable bringing up religion with my non-Christian
> friends. I valued my relationships and connections with them
> too much to introduce such a divisive topic. In many ways, it
> felt as if qualities that were part of my being an Asian woman
> were a liability for me.[7]

In addition to worrying about being a woman, Toyama also believed her Japanese ethnicity was a liability. The ways she related to
others—or was expected to relate to others—seemed contrary to
how she saw evangelism being done. She goes on to write about
doing conversational evangelism on the Berkeley campus as a
student, perhaps one of the scariest types of evangelism—beginning
spiritual conversations with complete strangers. Toyama describes
the anxiety she felt when her enthusiastic friend Grace invited her
to spend their lunch hour engaging people with the gospel. Grace
said a quick prayer and sent Toyama off by herself to talk to people
about Jesus. The fear of disappointing Grace spurred Toyama into
having conversations with people who were very open to sharing
their thoughts about Jesus and spirituality. She writes,

> Afterward, I spoke with Grace about my initial fears—that
> people would be angry that we're talking about God, that
> we're Christians; that people would feel offended.
>
> "Who would be scared or offended by *us*?" she said, ges-
> turing at her five-foot-tall persona.
>
> I looked down at my own five-foot frame. Part of what had
> opened the door to spiritual issues is that we don't look like
> stereotypical Christians to the campus. We could make chal-

lenging statements and people didn't feel threatened. We could talk about heaven and hell in a way that my five-foot-ten, Caucasian colleague could never do on our politically correct campus.

I laughed—Grace was right. My Asian culture had given me two gifts that could be used well for evangelism—a gracious way of bringing up hard topics and an unimposing reputation.[8]

Just like Nikki Toyama, you are exactly the woman God created you to be. It *will* be painful and confusing to work through racism, sexism, sizeism, ageism and all the other isms that seem to block your way in sharing Jesus. But he is with you in it all. He is able to guide you and guard you in the adventure of witness.

Response

Have there been times in your life when you were embarrassed or ashamed to be a woman? When have you been worried that something about your physical body—your ethnicity, your style, your size—would be a hindrance to witness? Pray and confess these areas to God as they fill your memory. Ask Jesus to show you where he was during these times and to heal you of the pain from these encounters. Ask Jesus to show you how he sees you, then receive the picture, song or Scriptures he may give you as a reminder that you are fearfully and wonderfully made.

Fashionistas for Jesus

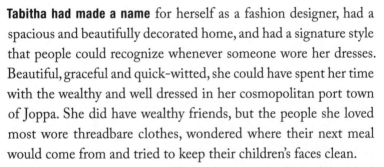

Tabitha had made a name for herself as a fashion designer, had a spacious and beautifully decorated home, and had a signature style that people could recognize whenever someone wore her dresses. Beautiful, graceful and quick-witted, she could have spent her time with the wealthy and well dressed in her cosmopolitan port town of Joppa. She did have wealthy friends, but the people she loved most wore threadbare clothes, wondered where their next meal would come from and tried to keep their children's faces clean.

In Acts 9, where we find Tabitha's story, the Holy Spirit had begun to move believers out into the world to share the gospel. The barriers between Jews and Gentiles, rich and poor, and men and women were beginning to break down. The people of God were demonstrating what it means to live as Jesus' disciples. Tabitha's story illustrates how the gospel transforms relationships and communities.

It's easy to skip over Tabitha's story, which is sandwiched between Saul's dramatic conversion and Peter's rooftop vision of eating unclean food as a symbol of God breaking down barriers between Jews and Gentiles. Tabitha's story seems unremarkable in the midst of these two stories, but the author, Luke, made a point to highlight her faith and service that led many others to Jesus. Tabitha's life and ministry as a fashion designer were important to the mission of God, so much so that he raised her back to life to continue to help others know about him. The story of Tabitha demonstrates that caring about clothing and external appearance is valuable to the mission of God when used to serve the needs of others.

> The story of Tabitha demonstrates that caring about clothing and external appearance is valuable to the mission of God when used to serve the needs of others.

In Joppa there was a disciple named Tabitha (in Greek her name is Dorcas); she was always doing good and helping the poor. About that time she became sick and died, and her body was washed and placed in an upstairs room. Lydda was near Joppa; so when the disciples heard that Peter was in Lydda, they sent two men to him and urged him, "Please come at once!"

Peter went with them, and when he arrived he was taken upstairs to the room. All the widows stood around him, crying and showing him the robes and other clothing that Dorcas had made while she was still with them.

Peter sent them all out of the room; then he got down on his knees and prayed. Turning toward the dead woman, he said, "Tabitha, get up." She opened her eyes, and seeing Peter she sat up. He took her by the hand and helped her to her feet. Then he called for the believers, especially the widows, and presented her to them alive. This became known all over Joppa, and many people believed in the Lord. Peter stayed in Joppa for some time with a tanner named Simon. (Acts 9:36-43)

Radical Hospitality

Tabitha welcomed poor and widowed women into her home when

they would otherwise have little hope that anyone would care for them. Some were too old to be married, others were fearful that they would be taken advantage of in their destitute state. Yet in Tabitha's home, they felt welcomed, never judged.

Imagine a young widow leading her noisy children into Tabitha's home, worrying that they were going to break something. Tabitha probably set out a snack and a few toys for the kids to play with so she could have a real conversation with this tired, overwhelmed widow. Maybe she poured tea for both of them and then listened as the widow told her story. Tears may have welled up in Tabitha's eyes as she heard about the husband's sudden death, the unjust plight of the widow not being able to own property. Like thousands of Israelite widows before her, this widow would have known how dangerously close she was to slipping through the cracks of society, to being forced to sell herself and her children into slavery for basic necessities like food, clothing and shelter. Perhaps Tabitha smiled and said, "Honey, let me whip you up a fabulous outfit."

It is easy to take clothing for granted. But for a widow and her children who were on the margins of society, staying clothed kept them one step away from being homeless or needing to resort to slavery.

In her article "My Sister's Keeper," Lynne Hybels writes about her experiences of growing compassion for marginalized women around the world. Orphans and widows live in our midst today in Africa, Eastern Europe, South America, China and the United States. There is not one country where women don't face the horror of crushing poverty. Hybels writes, "In an urban slum we met a beautiful young mother, widowed by AIDS, who had sold herself into prostitution because in a area with 98% unemployment, there was no other way for her to feed her children."[1]

Tabitha's story of radical hospitality and love for the poor and widowed isn't a sentimental ancient text. It's a call for women today to act with compassion and care for the orphans and widows in our neighborhoods, cities and world. These sisters are suffering. Tabitha shared the heart of Jesus for these women and opened her home. She used her resources and her skills to do something to make a difference in their lives. She didn't just offer them clothing, she offered them friendship, empathy and a social connection with other women who supported each other to ensure that all of them were cared for.

Tabitha served and loved the poor. James 1:27 says, "Religion that God our Father accepts as pure and faultless is this: to look after orphans and widows in their distress and to keep oneself from being polluted by the world." Tabitha managed to do both. She not only cared for the poor and widowed in her community, but she also made a choice to do so when she could have lived very differently. Joppa was a port town, cosmopolitan because it had lots of different types of people trading goods. If you picture the New York fashion scene, Tabitha would have been a top-tier designer who could have made a fortune exporting her clothing or selling it to the wealthy of Joppa.

It's easy to become polluted by the world. The temptations Tabitha would have faced in Joppa aren't much different than what we face today: clothing, food, jewelry, a beautiful home, the draw of powerful and well-connected friends. It's tempting and effortless to spend hours on Pinterest pinning our dream homes, vacations, healthy recipes or coordinated outfits, and forgetting that we have sisters suffering across the world. We can insulate ourselves from their pain and cries for help or we can do something about it. Tabitha is a radical example of a disciple who used what she had to care for the women God put around her. She didn't need to go anywhere to serve Jesus. She just had to open her eyes and her heart. She used her home as a resource to put her faith into action. This is why we need to follow Jesus in community. It's too easy for us to take our eyes off Jesus and be overcome with our desires instead of overcome with compassion.

Tabitha died and was resurrected. Tabitha became sick and died suddenly. Peter was in a nearby town and two men were sent to bring him to Tabitha's home. It's clear that her death hugely affected her community. It made a difference that she was gone. The widows mourned. They mobbed Peter to show him the clothing she made for them (Acts 9:39).

My pastor, Scott, often asks our motley congregation, "If our church left this community, would it make a difference? If you left your neighborhood or job, would people be worse off because you were gone? Our neighborhoods and cities should experience the love of Jesus because we are here and we serve them in practical ways." And then he recruits us to volunteer for something practical like stuffing new backpacks full of school supplies for kids whose parents can't afford to buy one when the new school year starts. Scott couples a call to action with a practical way to serve a need in our community.

Tabitha was already dead: "Her body was washed and placed in an upstairs room" (Acts 9:37). She wasn't like other sick people in the New Testament—the woman with perpetual bleeding or the demon-possessed slave girl. She was *dead*. After sending the weeping widows out of the room, Peter knelt down in the quiet room to pray. He turned to God for the power of the resurrection through the Holy Spirit and spoke a simple instruction, "Tabitha, get up." Nothing dramatic happened, just prayer and the instruction to get up. Yet through the power of Jesus, death was reversed into life. Through Peter and the beginnings of the early church, Jesus' words were coming true: "Very truly I tell you, whoever believes in me will do the works I have been doing, and they will do even greater things than these, because I am going to the Father" (John 14:12).

What was so special about Tabitha that she was raised from the dead? Peter presented her alive to the believers—the passage says "especially the widows" (Acts 9:41). Tabitha's resurrection did some amazing things. It demonstrated to the widows that God loved them enough to raise back to life their friend and advocate. God saw her mission as important. He answered Peter's prayers for her to be raised from the dead. Let that sink in for a minute. God raised a fashion designer back to life because she was strategic in Jesus' mission to care for the widows and the poor. When was the last time you heard a sermon preached about that? Widows and wealthy fashion designers are equally important in the kingdom of God.

> God raised a fashion designer back to life because she was strategic in Jesus' mission to care for the widows and the poor.

Revival broke out in Joppa. News of Tabitha's resurrection spread all over Joppa. Again, think about what it would be like if a New York City fashion designer who cared for the poor was raised from the dead. It would be endlessly broadcasted. Tabitha was not only a fashion designer, but she was also a disciple who had likely been leading a house church in her large home for the poor and widowed women. Her faith in Jesus enabled her to love and lead after she was raised from the dead to help hundreds of others begin to follow him. She had the character, resources and alignment with God's mission to not just send fabulous clothing out from the port of Joppa. She sent out the good news that Jesus is alive and able to give us new life.

Everything Is Missional

It's a shame that Tabitha's story gets glossed over, because her life, skills and ministry paint a picture of being equal in Jesus regardless of socioeconomic status or gender. A wealthy woman made clothes for the poor. This is a stark contrast to the women who work in sweatshops around the world to bring us five-dollar shirts at big-box stores in the United States. Tabitha's love of Jesus compelled her to make clothing that restored dignity and beauty to marginalized women. What we do with our stuff matters. How we use our stuff to care for others matters even more.

Often we feel like we have so little to offer others in service of Jesus. I have heard countless times, "I'm just a college student," "I'm just a stay-at-home mom," "I'm just a barista," "What can I do to actually make a difference in the world?" If we take anything from Tabitha's story, it is that anything we do can be done in service of our Lord Jesus. We can start small: Being generous instead of hoarding. Seeking to provide for others instead of seeing how much we can get for ourselves. Beginning to see as missional those things that we have deemed trivial. Let's face it, the church often dismisses clothing, makeup and jewelry as trifling, but Tabitha's story illustrates that stuff isn't bad. God uses physical things to demonstrate to others that he loves them. These poor and widowed women needed what Tabitha provided back then, and the poor and widowed of today need what we can provide.

There are women who need help learning how to cook healthy foods on a food-stamp budget, to dress for a job interview after being rescued from human trafficking, to have a place to exercise and lead a healthy lifestyle amid rural poverty, and to feel beautiful, valued and loved not because of what they offer to society but because God loves them deeply.

There are women who need help learning how to cook healthy foods on a food-stamp budget, to dress for a job interview after being rescued from human trafficking, to have a place to exercise and lead a healthy lifestyle amid rural poverty, and to feel beautiful, valued and loved not because of what they offer to society but because God loves them deeply.

The Priestess of Lipstick

We aren't surrounded by only the physically poor; we are also surrounded by the spiritually poor. We would be compartmentalizing God's mission if we only understood it as calling us to serve women in physical poverty. The wealthy and well connected can also live in poverty—a poverty of relationships, connection with God and purpose in life beyond consumerism.

My sister, Rachel, is a missionary to these kinds of impoverished women. Though I love to visit Rachel to get my makeup done at the upscale boutique where she manages the makeup counter, I love even more the stories about the women she interacts with. Over the years, she has told me countless experiences of praying for women who come in for a makeover and leave realizing how much God loves them. She sees her role at the boutique as an ambassador of the love of Jesus, not just someone who sells expensive facial cream. Though these women come in to try on five-thousand-dollar dresses and buy tubes of three-hundred-dollar moisturizer, after interacting with Rachel, they leave believing that they are worth more than how they clothe themselves or the products they buy. When they sit down with Rachel, she gently touches their face to apply lipstick and mascara and does so as God's image bearer. She silently prays for them. Women who are depressed, trying to prove their worth by what they wear, feeling insecure in their abilities or going through a painful divorce begin to realize that buying designer clothing and upscale makeup does not bring them life. They may not be materially poor, but so many are living in spiritual poverty.[2]

One woman who had just separated from her husband and was worried about what it would do to her two kids said to my sister during a makeover event, "I was going to stay home tonight and drink a bottle of wine and read a magazine by myself. I'm so glad I came out for this makeover event and that you offered to pray with me." Rachel had just prayed with her client to recommit her life to Jesus. Since then, she has helped this woman get connected with a church and grow in her relationship with Jesus.

Though it is unlikely that Rachel will ever hear a sermon preached about the strategic nature of her work to an unreached mission field of wealthy fashion lovers, she indeed works as a missionary in an industry that is typically dismissed by the church as petty, materialistic and unspiritual. She is caring for women to help them realize that God loves them just as they are.

The ways women connect with each other are often seen as trivial. Many of us get excited about a shimmering new lip gloss that moisturizes but isn't sticky, jeans that actually fit and make your butt look good, a killer pair of running shoes with magenta and yellow accents that make you feel fierce as you care for your body. Tara, my friend who works as a restoration carpenter, once gushed to me about what a pretty blue her new welding helmet was. I made fun of her for that for a long time. But even a welding helmet can make you feel more like the woman God has made you to be.

Image Bearers

We are image bearers of the living God. So it makes sense that our visual world—including the clothes we choose to cover ourselves— matters. As Jesus' witnesses, we must demonstrate what it means to be a disciple of Jesus as well as speak about it and serve in his name. The temptation for most women is to not speak up, but to hope that somewhere along the line, their friends will catch that they follow Jesus. It's essential, however, to tell the stories of why we live the way we do. Just like Tabitha, the love of Jesus compels us.

In their book *Untamed: Reactivating a Missional Form of Discipleship*, authors Alan and Deb Hirsch share a story about friends from church inviting their non-Christian friends to have a "Stitch 'n' Bitch" night to knit and connect with each other.[3] Early on the group decided that they wouldn't just enjoy time together but that they would also serve their community. Since Deb's house was near the red-light district and it was the middle of winter, they began knitting sexy scarves for the local working girls. This wasn't a group of condemning church ladies telling the prostitutes to cover themselves with grandma-style scarves; rather, it was a genuine expression of love to communicate, "We know you are cold and you want to look good. We can help with both of those things." It was their compassion and service that provided a place for their non-Christian friends to experientially explore what it meant to be a disciple of Jesus. The Hirsches write,

> Our discipling of them was to expose them to the values of the kingdom and the heart of Jesus for the outcast.... Most of these women started as professional women concerned with becoming affluent, getting bigger and better homes, and living more comfortable lifestyles. Discipling for them meant that over time they began to look more like Jesus by embracing values that were more in line with the kingdom, and as this transformation began, questions about God and Jesus started taking place.[4]

Over time, the group of non-Christian women began to see the values of the kingdom of God by serving the marginalized, building relationships, serving others together and providing for a practical need.

Just as Tabitha and Deb and her church friends did, we can invite others to participate in the mission of God, to experience what it is like to follow Jesus. This can include simple things. A compliment on your necklace or scarf can turn into a conversation about how it was made by rescued sex slaves in Thailand. Curiosity can be piqued and a conversation can turn into an invitation to serve others in your community. An invitation to knit scarves for prostitutes, serve the needs of single moms or sit and listen to widowed women can lead to exploration of Jesus. And exploration of Jesus and living out his teachings in community can lead to salvation.

This was what happened in Joppa for so many people because of Tabitha's example. And her faith is what Jesus calls us to emulate— faith that demonstrates God's compassion in practical ways, lives out radical hospitality and uses the resources we have to invite others into the mission of God so that they begin to follow Jesus as well.

Response

Who are the poor and marginalized in your community? Look online to find places where homeless or battered women, single moms, or refugee families are served. Get your campus group or church to volunteer or donate needed items to these places.

Who are the spiritually poor with whom you interact? What have they shared with you about places in their lives where they feel empty, unsatisfied, alone or depressed? Offer to pray with and for them. Invite them to church or to come and serve with you in caring for the marginalized.

What is your tendency when faced with stories of women in poverty? Despair? Escape? Activism? Pray that Jesus will lead you and your community into love, compassion and action.

First-Date Awkwardness

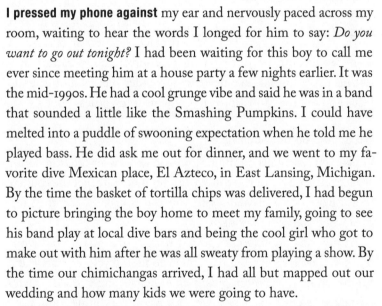

I pressed my phone against my ear and nervously paced across my room, waiting to hear the words I longed for him to say: *Do you want to go out tonight?* I had been waiting for this boy to call me ever since meeting him at a house party a few nights earlier. It was the mid-1990s. He had a cool grunge vibe and said he was in a band that sounded a little like the Smashing Pumpkins. I could have melted into a puddle of swooning expectation when he told me he played bass. He did ask me out for dinner, and we went to my favorite dive Mexican place, El Azteco, in East Lansing, Michigan. By the time the basket of tortilla chips was delivered, I had begun to picture bringing the boy home to meet my family, going to see his band play at local dive bars and being the cool girl who got to make out with him after he was all sweaty from playing a show. By the time our chimichangas arrived, I had all but mapped out our wedding and how many kids we were going to have.

It's been a long time since I've obsessively waited for a boy to call and ask me on a date now that I've been married to my sexy, bearded husband for over a decade. Dating is scary because so much of the relationship is out of our control. We imagine how we want things to play out, but ultimately the spark of love is not something we can create. It happens with some people easily, but it takes a long time for others. And for some people, it never happens at all, despite lots of opportunities to connect.

Though I haven't neurotically planned out a relationship with a guy in years, I have done so in relationships where I was seeking to share Jesus with others. I can become like the obnoxious matchmaker trying to connect people to Jesus: "Seriously, you should just hang out with him once. He has the best personality and is an amazing listener!" There's nothing wrong with trying to connect friends with Jesus. That's what we're meant to do as his followers.

> I can become like the obnoxious matchmaker trying to connect people to Jesus: "Seriously, you should just hang out with him once."

The problem is when we obsessively turn people into projects, trying to control things rather than letting them unfold. We need to surrender our relationships to Jesus and ask the Holy Spirit to guide us into witness.

We Should Go Out Sometime

When you have kids, finding mom friends is a lot like the dating scene. You see a mom you think you'd hit it off with, get the courage to ask her to do a playdate with you and your kids, and then feel cool when you score her digits.

At my son's preschool, I spotted Kim on the playground while our preschoolers ran around us. She had motorcycle-chic style and bright red hair. The mom pickup lines began, and a few days later, we talked as our sons played with trains on her dining room floor. Kim shared with me about her spiritual life and background after I asked if she and her husband attended church anywhere. I noticed an Eckhart Tolle book and a book about world religions on her built-in bookcase. The titles echoed what she had shared over coffee: she and her husband were spiritual but not religious.

As we talked, my mind started spinning over how to help her meet Jesus. I pictured her and her family showing up to our church for the first time and being wowed by how welcome they felt and what a cool worship band we had. I imagined hunkering over more cups of coffee at our local coffee shop as we explored Jesus' teachings together. I pictured her and her husband sitting on their couch and earnestly praying to invite Jesus to lead their lives. I became that creepy girl mapping out how I wanted our relationship and Kim's relationship with Jesus to play out. In those weeks, I'm sad to say, I forgot that Kim was a real live person with choices and fears. She probably had a "this person is getting weird" detector go off at a certain point in our relationship. You can tell when someone is way more into you than you are into them, and it feels uncomfortable.

I'm terrified of being lumped in with negative stereotypes of pushy evangelists. Up there with discovering that there are sharks in the Great Lakes or that one of my sons will die, being labeled a pushy evangelist is in my top five fears.[1] When it was clear that Kim and I weren't going to be best buds or even hang out on a regular basis, I let the relationship go. There was nothing more I could do. I felt sad, ashamed and embarrassed that I had let our relationship become forced in my mind. I spent some time in prayer. I confessed my independence from Jesus and my disappointment that I wasn't going to see if her relationship with Jesus would develop. I repented of my desire to control things rather than trusting the Holy Spirit to work in Kim's heart at his own pace. I prayed Jesus would use the gospel seeds I had scattered in her life to help her take steps toward him and that her family would eventually invite Jesus to be the leader of their lives.

Sowing the Seeds of Love

The parable of the sower has been a seminal passage in my life. Jesus has used it to remind me that the destiny of people's souls has very little to do with what I say or do. I can be faithful to sow gospel seeds, but the Holy Spirit enables those seeds to grow and bear a fruitful, vibrant relationship with Jesus.

As they went from town to town, a lot of people joined in and traveled along. He addressed them, using this story: "A farmer went out to sow his seed. Some of it fell on the road; it was tramped down and the birds ate it. Other seed fell in the gravel; it sprouted, but withered because it didn't have good roots. Other seed fell in the weeds; the weeds grew with it and strangled it. Other seed fell in rich earth and produced a bumper crop.

"Are you listening to this? Really listening?"

His disciples asked, "Why did you tell this story?"

He said, "You've been given insight into God's kingdom— you know how it works. There are others who need stories. But even with stories some of them aren't going to get it:

> Their eyes are open but don't see a thing,
> Their ears are open but don't hear a thing.

"This story is about some of those people. The seed is the Word of God. The seeds on the road are those who hear the Word, but no sooner do they hear it than the Devil snatches it from them so they won't believe and be saved.

"The seeds in the gravel are those who hear with enthusiasm, but the enthusiasm doesn't go very deep. It's only another fad, and the moment there's trouble it's gone.

"And the seed that fell in the weeds—well, these are the ones who hear, but then the seed is crowded out and nothing comes of it as they go about their lives worrying about tomorrow, making money, and having fun.

"But the seed in the good earth—these are the good-hearts

who seize the Word and hold on no matter what, sticking with it until there's a harvest." (Luke 8:4-15 *The Message*)

I remember a particularly difficult encounter sharing Jesus with a student on campus who was sitting next to me, studying. As we engaged in conversation, I eventually shared the gospel and she began to look at me like I had a third eyeball growing out of my forehead. She abruptly ended our conversation and scurried away with her backpack while I sat in the overstuffed leather chair with my face reddening. I felt like a freak and wondered, *What's the point of any of this if I'm just going to look stupid and feel terrible after I share Jesus with people?* Disheartened, I drove home to eat lunch between meetings and sensed the Lord inviting me to spend time with him in Scripture. I sat down with a ham sandwich and my Bible and found myself reading the parable of the sower.

The Holy Spirit pointed a couple things out to me: "See, you have no control over what someone's heart is like when you share the gospel. That is entirely up to me! Don't feel bad. You did what you're supposed to do: scatter the gospel seeds. It's precisely because you don't know what's going on in people's hearts that you need to throw all the seed you can out there. Do you realize the odds Jesus was facing? One in four ended up producing a harvest! He preached to the crowds knowing all the while that most of what he shared wouldn't be received." I pushed my chair away from the table and looked out the window. I pictured Jesus preaching to large crowds, knowing that the gospel seeds he was scattering would get trampled, wither up and be strangled by weeds. I thought about how it must have grieved him to know this. I thought about the love he had to keep going out to scatter the gospel seeds so that some would embrace the Father. As I looked at the oak trees swaying above my neighbors' rooftops, the Holy Spirit seemed to say to me, "Little Jessica, you don't know what God can and wants to do in the heart of any person you meet. Just keep scattering the gospel seeds with thankfulness that I do the work of producing fruit, not you."

Harvest Dreams

Evangelism is a mysterious process led by the Spirit, not by us. What is clear to us is that we're meant to build relationships and scatter seeds of the gospel liberally. Even if we have no idea what God has done and is doing in our friends' lives, the Holy Spirit is able to guide us into the next appropriate ways to help them meet Jesus. We can joyfully anticipate all the ways God is wooing our friends into relationship with him, yet prayerfully surrender control as we trust him to do the work only he can do. It's good to dream, but we can't take things into our own hands.

Blogger Anna Gissing, in her reflections on the parable of the sower, writes,

> As I thought about the farmer, I realized the end result would not have been my focus. I'd have been annoyed that I had wasted that other seed—the seed that the birds ate, the sun scorched, and the thorns choked. What about that seed? How could I have avoided that loss? The wasted seed weighed heavy on my heart. And I realized that describes my own resistance to risk. Afraid that all of the seed sown won't be fruitful, I hold onto the seed. I won't waste it if I don't throw it on the path or in the rocky or thorny soil. Yet, I also don't throw it in the good soil. I don't throw it at all. But what good is it to hang onto the seed and never sow it? At harvest time, I will have nothing. No fruit to show because there was no labor; no joy at the growth.[2]

We never know how seed will grow when it is scattered. Evangelism is the mystifying coalescence of our action and God's action.

More important than dreaming about how friends will meet Jesus, we can ask God to make these dreams a reality. He dreams and longs for this to be true in our friends' lives far more often and earnestly than we ever could.

In contrast with my story with Kim, I immediately hit it off with my friend Joey, who showed up at a summer playdate our MOPS

> Evangelism is the mystifying coalescence of our action and God's action.

(Mothers of Preschoolers) group hosted. Joey was easygoing, funny and real. She laughed and joked easily, even as she wrangled her sweet, redheaded daughter and energetic son to slather sunscreen on them before they dashed off to play in the sprinklers at the splash park. On future playdates, we shared our gratitude for the wonders of Prozac in our struggles with depression, our spiritual backgrounds and the latest ways to cook the zucchini that was growing prolifically in Cleveland that August.

I dreamed of what God would do in Joey's life, but mostly I prayed, "Jesus, help me trust you with the next steps you are inviting Joey to take with you. Show me how you want me to care for her." Our MOPS group prayed for her as well. We loved her, hung out, had fun together and talked about spiritual things as they came up or were brought up in a natural way. About six months into our relationship, we scheduled a moms' night out. I felt it could be an ideal time to share the gospel with her since we wouldn't be chasing our kids around. I prayed that God would open her heart to re-spond to the gospel during our time together. I prayed that I wouldn't be weird and awkward about it and that I wouldn't chicken out. Over mouthfuls of caramel-smothered cheesecake at the Cheesecake Factory, we caught up on our holidays and talked about MOPS.

I brought up the topic of her spiritual life.

"My mom is an agnostic," Joey said, "and my husband isn't interested in going to church. I've been to all sorts of churches. I went to temple with a friend and then a Black Pentecostal church a couple years later. I loved the gospel music!"

I tentatively asked Joey if she had heard the basic message of what it means to follow Jesus. When she responded that she hadn't, I asked if I could share it with her using an app called The Big Story, which my friend Sarah helped develop with InterVarsity. I had recently downloaded the app and was still getting comfortable using it. I didn't feel entirely prepared to use it that night but thought I would give it a try. After we talked about the message of Jesus in the app, Joey continued to share about her family and her desire to know more about God.

I asked, "Is what I just shared about Jesus something you want for your life?" Looking at me directly, her hands folded and her half-eaten cheesecake pushed to the side, Joey smiled and said, "Yes! This is what I want!" That night, the Cheesecake Factory was holy ground as Joey prayed to begin following Jesus. We talked about the next steps to grow her relationship with Jesus, and she downloaded the app on her phone.

She smiled and shook her head. "People are going to give me crap about becoming a Christian."

"What about becoming a Christian?" I asked, recalling a heated Facebook thread on her page about whether Christians actually voted Democrat.

"Well," she continued, "I have some pretty liberal views. Even though I'm fine with other people disagreeing with me, I just don't know if I can go along with some of the more conservative things."

"Joey, the amazing thing about following Jesus is that it doesn't matter to him how you vote, how you dress, what your past has been like or the things you're struggling with now. He loves you, just as you are. You don't have to clean up or do any special thing to accept him. He wants you to become the person God has created you to be and care for this world in the way that only you can."

Joey's eyes opened wide. "Really?!"

I smiled and nodded. "Yep."

"Huh," she leaned back in her seat. "Why don't more people know about this?"

I smiled wider. "That's the best part, Joey. We get to tell other people about what it really means to follow Jesus! And we get to follow him in all the diverse ways he created us to be."

"Yeah," she said, "if I saw you across the restaurant, I wouldn't think, *She looks like a Christian.*"

Though this might have offended some people, I cracked up.

"People think you have to completely change who you are when you become a Christian," I said. "But Jesus knows I'm a goofy person who loves fashion and pop culture, and that's fine with him. He loves how he created me and he loves how he created you!"

As I drove home, I thought about Joey's question: *Why don't more people know about this?* It made me hope and pray that Joey would be a Jesus follower who shared his story with others. As with Kim, I had no idea where my relationship with Joey would lead. But as I spent time getting to know her and praying for her, it was clear that Jesus was inviting me to take a risk in sharing the gospel with her and inviting her to respond.

The Next Appropriate Risk

We can begin with the end in mind: Jesus is always moving in his mission to seek and save the lost. And we can trust him to lead us as we look for the next appropriate step to encourage friends and strangers to seek and follow him. Sometimes the next appropriate risk is simply to acknowledge that God is inviting us to join him in loving others and ask him how he would have us respond. Some people you encounter every day may be waiting for a person to tell them about what it means to follow Jesus. Others may have a hard time trusting Christians because of negative experiences they've had. We don't know where people are unless we ask them questions. Asking people about their experiences, desires and frustrations can help you avoid awkwardness, fear and confusion about where someone is spiritually. Then you can prayerfully ask the Holy Spirit what the next appropriate risk is to invite them to explore Jesus.

Years ago I asked Todd, a friend of mine who wouldn't consider himself religious or spiritual, to listen to a sermon I preached and give me feedback. I had an assignment for a class on preaching at Wheaton Graduate School, which became a great opportunity to invite my friend to listen to me share the gospel, though we lived on opposite sides of the country. Because he was someone who didn't go to church and wasn't interested, I wanted to hear what he thought about the message of Jesus and if what I shared made sense to him. He ended up listening to it with his friends at work and launching into an amazing discussion with them about their spiritual backgrounds! Because I took a risk, Todd had an opportunity for a discussion with his friends about an important area of life. We can feel uncomfortable bringing up spiritual things with others out of the blue. Yet seemingly mundane activities, like a project you're working on, the books you're reading or the movies you're watching, can become great opportunities to begin a spiritual conversation.

Response

Who are people you interact with on a regular basis? Women in your residence hall or classes, in your neighborhood, at your workplace or volunteer event? Spend some time praying for one of them right now. Ask Jesus to give you insight into caring for her and serving her in practical ways.

Send a text message to a friend who is far from God and ask if you can grab lunch or coffee with her. When you do get together, ask her about her spiritual background by saying something like, "You know, we know a lot about each other but I've never asked—What's your spiritual background?" It's amazing that people can know each other for a long time and have never asked this question! Or, if it's a person you haven't known for long, you can say something like, "I've been reading this book about women's spiritual lives—have you ever had any experiences you'd consider spiritual?" Her answer will give you some sort of insight into her beliefs, whether or not she currently goes to church, or if she's interested in talking more about spiritual things—and it will give you an opportunity to share about any spiritual experiences you've had.

Choose the Right Shoes

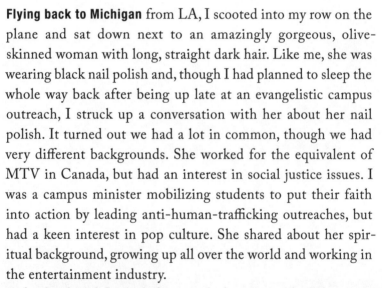

Flying back to Michigan from LA, I scooted into my row on the plane and sat down next to an amazingly gorgeous, olive-skinned woman with long, straight dark hair. Like me, she was wearing black nail polish and, though I had planned to sleep the whole way back after being up late at an evangelistic campus outreach, I struck up a conversation with her about her nail polish. It turned out we had a lot in common, though we had very different backgrounds. She worked for the equivalent of MTV in Canada, but had an interest in social justice issues. I was a campus minister mobilizing students to put their faith into action by leading anti-human-trafficking outreaches, but had a keen interest in pop culture. She shared about her spiritual background, growing up all over the world and working in the entertainment industry.

As she shared, I asked if anyone had ever prayed a blessing on her and her work.

"No, there aren't a lot of Christians in the entertainment industry," she replied, laughing a bit and surprised by my question.

I offered to pray for her as we descended into Chicago and asked God to use her and her influence to help others care for the world.

As we touched down, she thanked me and we clicked through our Facebook apps to become friends.

As we were leaving the plane, she said, "We need more Christians like you and your people out there. You're getting a bad rap." I laughed, thanked her and assured her that there were a lot of Christians like me who cared about following Jesus and demonstrating our faith in practical ways.

A few years later, I was watching a then-new show with Zooey Deschanel called *New Girl*, when that same beautiful, olive-skinned woman, Hannah Simone, came on the screen as the character CeCe. I pointed and yelled to my husband, "I know her! I prayed for her on the airplane!"

My husband looked at me with confusion. "What airplane?"

I regaled him with the story once more and then asked God again to bless her and use the little interaction on that flight to draw her closer to Jesus.

Best. Outfit. Ever.

What seemed trivial with Hannah Simone actually ended up being a way to connect with her and strike up a conversation. Black nail polish became a connecting point for us. What we wear matters for the context we're in. Specifically, our shoes matter for the context we're in. I'm guessing that when you get ready for an event you want to dress for the occasion. If you're invited to a cocktail party, you're probably not going to show up in your sturdiest hiking boots. Similarly, if your friends have invited you to go camping, you're not going to tuck your cutest pair of red kitten heels into your backpack. What we wear matters for the context, yet we can be confident that we always have the best shoes for every occasion because of the apostle Paul's fashion consulting.

In Ephesians 6, Paul outlines the spiritual armor, reminding us that we are engaged in a spiritual battle. If you've never pictured yourself as a warrior, now is a good time to start.

> Finally, be strong in the Lord and in his mighty power. Put on the full armor of God, so that you can take your stand against the devil's schemes. For our struggle is not against flesh and blood, but against the rulers, against the authorities, against the powers of this dark world and against the spiritual forces of evil in the heavenly realms. Therefore put on the full armor of God, so that when the day of evil comes, you may be able to stand your ground, and after you have done everything, to stand. Stand firm then, with the belt of truth buckled around your waist, with the breastplate of righteousness in place, and with your feet fitted with the readiness that comes from the gospel of peace. In addition to all this, take up the shield of faith, with which you can extinguish all the flaming arrows of the evil one. Take the helmet of salvation and the sword of the Spirit, which is the word of God.
>
> And pray in the Spirit on all occasions with all kinds of prayers and requests. With this in mind, be alert and always keep on praying for all the Lord's people. (Ephesians 6:10-18)

The NIRV translates verse 15, "Wear on your feet what will prepare you to tell the good news of peace." Regardless of which shoes you select to go with your outfit, the most important ones are those that will prepare you to share Jesus with others. We need to be ready to go to the people and places Jesus calls us to even when we least expect it or it's inconvenient.

It's essential to pray and ask the Holy Spirit how he is inviting us to engage others with the gospel, to serve them and care for their needs physically and spiritually. Just like selecting an outfit or pair of shoes, when it comes to evangelism, we need to ask ourselves,

What is the appropriate thing for this context? Rather than fumbling around blindly hoping we'll connect with others, we listen to the Holy Spirit, who can answer that question and point us in the right direction. Sometimes that will be a small risk, like being willing to tell someone you go to church. Other times it will be a bigger risk, such as using your small business as a platform to share the gospel or explaining why you turned down a prestigious internship in favor of going on a mission trip.

Confession: I Am a Shoe Glutton

Marilyn Monroe is attributed to have said, "Give a girl the right shoes and she can conquer the world." At various points in my life I have been on quests to find the perfect shoes to walk into any and every situation with confidence. I can remember being fixated on a pair of black suede platform shoes from Macy's when I was in high school and begging my mom to take me to get them. She and my dad had planned on going on a date and weren't willing to let me tag along for my shoe quest. Undeterred, I traced an outline of my feet, thrust the paper in her hand and said, "Here, at least you'll have this to know which size I need." She returned a few hours later with a pair of size 7.5, black suede platform shoes. I triumphed and strutted around the living room modeling my new shoes. From scouring shops in London for biker-style Doc Martens to online shopping for bright Nike running shoes to start a new fitness routine, I like being able to have the right shoes for the right occasion. One pair of black flats will just not do to step into all the spheres Jesus has sent me into.

I Say a Little Prayer for You

God has given us lots of options for how to share Jesus, from engaging friends to preaching before thousands. No matter what we've been told about what types of evangelism women do best, we need to boldly and lovingly step out in how Jesus is calling us to share the gospel. It's likely that you are already doing many things that might enable you to share. We are wired for relationship, and relationship is what evangelism is all about—God's people extending his love to others no matter where they are spiritually.

Ephesians 6:18 tells us to "pray in the Spirit on all occasions with all kinds of prayers and requests." How often has someone shared with you about something difficult they're struggling with and you look at them with empathy and say, "Wow, that sounds rough. I'll pray for you about that." Though you have good intentions to pray about it, your mind gets filled with bills that arrived in the mail, what to make for dinner or the project you're trying to finish by the end of the week. You might feel powerless or lost as to how to help a stranger, friend or family member struggling with a major crisis. One of the most powerful ways to share Jesus with others is to actually pray for them on the spot, whether they are Christian or not. Offering to pray for someone who isn't a Christian is disarming because you are choosing to go before the God you believe in on behalf of your struggling friend. You aren't asking them to believe in the God in whom you believe; rather, you are inviting them into the presence of God *with* you to ask him to meet their needs. Often the way people experience God's care is through you, which deepens your relationship with them and provides a safe place for them to ask you questions.

We never know whom Jesus will put in our paths. Yet whomever we encounter, we have an opportunity to connect them to the source of life and hope: Jesus. I have prayed with and for women who are friends, strangers and acquaintances. I've prayed outside grocery stores for homeless women, at bed and breakfasts with businesswomen, on campuses, in my driveway and in the tiny kitchens of college apartments. Each time, the woman is touched that I would offer to pray for her and care for her. This act of love opens up the opportunity for future spiritual conversations and helps them experience the Holy Spirit's presence. Prayer provides a natural way to come back to the person and ask, "How is the situation we prayed about? I've continued to pray for you."

Because I've chosen to ask if I could pray with and for a person when they share their concerns, hurts or hopes, I've had non-Christian friends and neighbors regularly ask me to pray for them even though they have told me they don't believe in God, or aren't sure which god they believe in. From my simple step of obedience, the Holy Spirit begins to open hearts of people far from God to encounter Jesus. This is something any of us can do. We need only the willingness to offer to pray when someone shares about a hope or need they have in their life.

A few guidelines for praying for someone aloud who is far from God: Pray for them with simple language that they'll understand. Christians sometimes forget that not everyone knows all the jargon or "Christianese" in which we are fluent. Thank God for them, acknowledge what they're struggling with and ask Jesus to care for them and provide for their needs. Some people might have prayed before, but for others, it may be the first time having someone offer to pray *for* them. Explain to them how you'd like to pray, whether it's with your eyes closed, putting your hand on their shoulder or having them hold out their hands as a sign of openness to receive from God. This also helps the person feel comfortable and know what to expect during the experience. After you've prayed for them, follow up again to see how they're doing and listen for how God might be moving in their lives.

I once prayed for my Jewish Buddhist neighbor, Maureen, when she shared about being stressed out about her boyfriend's job search and how it had put a strain on their relationship. Standing on the sidewalk while my kids scooted around on their Big Wheels, I prayed something like this, "Jesus, thank you that you love

Maureen. Thank you that you care about her and see the ways she's trying to love her boyfriend. I pray that you would guide her in the best ways to love Tim in this difficult situation. Please give Tim a job. I pray for peace for Maureen and Tim while they wait as he looks for a job. Thank you that you love us and care about every area of our lives."

Love, peace, provision—most people are pretty comfortable with a prayer of blessing for these things. So why not let them know that Jesus cares for them and can guide them into all of these?

Come Sit at My Table

When was the last time you had someone over for a meal at your house? I'm not talking about a birthday party where you frantically cleaned to host a rowdy pack of eight-year-old kids and their families, or when you grabbed takeout and your roommate happened to be home while you ate pad thai. I'm talking about intentionally inviting someone to come into your space and share a meal. Though we text or tweet people thousands of miles away, we're often oblivious to the people God has placed right around us.

It's easy to make excuses about why it's inconvenient or uncomfortable to invite people into our homes and lives: your house or apartment isn't big enough or it's too messy; you can't afford anything fancy to feed people; it feels a little too intimate to have someone see what kind of art you like to hang on the walls, the books that line your shelves or whether you're a shoes-on or shoes-off type of house. But a profound thing happens spiritually when we invite someone to join us for a meal at our table. In Luke 19 when Jesus encounters Zacchaeus, the first thing Jesus does is demand to come to Zacchaeus's home and share a meal with him. Jesus is so bossy in this passage, as he sometimes can be when he wants to make a declarative statement of his love for someone.

Jesus entered Jericho and was passing through. A man was there by the name of Zacchaeus; he was a chief tax collector and was wealthy. He wanted to see who Jesus was, but because he was short he could not see over the crowd. So he ran ahead and climbed a sycamore-fig tree to see him, since Jesus was coming that way.

When Jesus reached the spot, he looked up and said to him, "Zacchaeus, come down immediately. I must stay at your house today." So he came down at once and welcomed him gladly.

All the people saw this and began to mutter, "He has gone to be the guest of a sinner."

But Zacchaeus stood up and said to the Lord, "Look, Lord! Here and now I give half of my possessions to the poor, and if I have cheated anybody out of anything, I will pay back four times the amount."

Jesus said to him, "Today salvation has come to this house, because this man, too, is a son of Abraham. For the Son of Man came to seek and to save the lost." (Luke 19:1-10)

Jesus invited himself over to Zacchaeus's house to demonstrate that he wanted to be part of his life. It didn't matter to Jesus what Zacchaeus had done or what others thought of him—Jesus wanted to enter his home, his world and his heart. To invite someone into the place we live indicates that we care more about the person than we do about what others will think of us, keeping up our appearances or opening ourselves up to judgment. People judged Jesus in this passage, muttering, "He has gone to be the guest of a sinner." Yet Jesus' initiative prompted Zacchaeus to turn from his greed and respond generously toward others.

It Doesn't Take Much

When my brother and sister and I were little, we would sing the

Zacchaeus song that many Christian kids learn. Except we would change the last line of the song, "for I'm coming to your house today," to, "for I'm coming to your house today to eat peanut butter and jelly." I don't know what Zacchaeus actually served Jesus, but I'm sure Jesus would have been content with something as simple as a PB&J. More important than what is served is a willingness to invite someone into your life and home so that they can encounter Jesus.

Beth noticed Lauren—the perfect-looking woman—every time she dropped her kids off at school. Lauren's car was always clean, her children were well dressed in the trendiest clothes, and she never showed up for drop-off in her yoga pants and an old T-shirt . . . unless, of course, she was on her way to work out, and then she had on a perfectly coordinated workout top with her yoga pants and cool athletic shoes.

Beth resented Lauren as she brushed the Cheerios and dried-up french fry remnants out of her own car after her kids scooted out the door. She felt self-conscious about the makeup-free dark circles under her eyes. It seemed like Lauren had everything together: perfect body, perfect kids and perfect home. As she was driving home, she began to feel sorry for herself and the pile of dishes awaiting her in the sink. "I'll bet Lauren never has a cereal bowl in the sink when she leaves to drop off her kids," she muttered. Then the Holy Spirit convicted her. "Beth, why do you think her life is perfect? She needs Jesus just like you do. Why don't you stop comparing yourself to her and begin praying for her?" Booyah. Holy Spirit for the win.

It took a little while, but as Beth began to pray for Lauren, her heart began to shift. It shifted from being self-conscious about how she wasn't like Lauren to how she could demonstrate Jesus' love to her. One morning as they were standing around watching their preschoolers on the playground, Beth took a risk and invited Lauren over for lunch.

"Not anything fancy, you know," Beth said self-consciously. "Just, like, grilled cheese."

Lauren's face broke into a smile. "We would love that! Thanks so much for the invite."

As Lauren sat at Beth's table while the kids played in the next room, she began to share how lonely she felt because her husband traveled for work so much. It hadn't been easy moving away from their family when they had relocated to Kansas City earlier that year. Beth decided to steer the conversation into spiritual matters as she buttered slices of bread for the grilled cheese. "Not sure if this is your thing, but have you guys found a church to attend yet?" Beth asked. Lauren shared how she had grown up in the church but never really felt connected, and that her husband's schedule made it difficult for them to attend services together as a family. Beth's heart began to pound as she flipped the sandwiches, her back turned to Lauren.

"I don't know if you'd be interested," she said as a caveat, "but would you like to come to church with us this week?" Beth's face cringed as she waited for the answer to her risky question. She turned to hand Lauren the plate of gooey grilled cheese as Lauren smiled and said, "I would love that. I've been wanting to find a church to take the kids to, but haven't known where to start."

We often assume that people aren't interested in Jesus or in church because we're afraid to step out and take a risk. We compare ourselves to other women in our dorm, neighborhood or workplace and immediately assume what their spiritual lives are like. We have no idea what the Holy Spirit is doing within the women and men around us. All we can do is ask them and pray that they'll respond. It can feel risky inviting people into our lives and asking them questions, but in doing so we demonstrate that we care for them and are interested in their lives. My friend Deborah once said to me, "I'd been waiting for someone to ask me about my spiritual life and where I was at with God. I'm thankful you actually asked me. It can be scary to bring those things up. I didn't know how to talk about how I'd walked away from God after my dad died, but because you asked and listened, it made a way for me to come back to God."

The Story of My Life

Often when I hear sermons, I can't remember the Scripture passage that was preached. However, if a powerful story accompanies the passage, or if the preacher has done an eloquent job helping me see the story in Scripture, it stays in my mind. We are storytellers of the gospel. You may feel like you don't have a story, but each one of us does.

My testimony is pretty unremarkable. I grew up in a Christian home and accepted Jesus through the Awana program as a child. In high school, I was interested in both youth-group fun and drinking and smoking in the woods with friends on the weekends. As a teenager I would be telling friends about the love of Jesus while taking swigs of Zima, the popular malt beverage of the early 1990s.[1] In college I spent most of my freshman year on a sin spree. I had intended to find poetry slams to attend, but I soon found myself at the keg parties on Beal Street, wearing skintight silver vinyl pants (inspired by the Spice Girls) and making out with boys who told me about their fascinating anthropology studies.

Toward the end of my freshman year, I was ashamed at my choices, disgusted to see the empty Popov vodka bottles sitting atop my dusty Bible and wondering why it was so difficult to make myself read that Bible. I had been to church a few times during the year but the Holy Spirit had been convicting me more and more that I wasn't living into the person God made me to be. That summer I went home to work on the grounds crew of a golf course and sort through what a mess of a year I'd had. Bored one night and looking for something to read, I found a copy of Watchman Nee's *The Normal Christian Life* on my parents' bookshelf. As I read, the Holy Spirit began to open my heart to what life with Christ was intended to be, and I wondered, *Why hasn't anyone ever told me this?!*

My parents had moved from the Upper Peninsula of Michigan to Grand Rapids after I graduated from high school, so I was extremely lonely since I didn't know anyone, and I was looking for places to make friends. My parents suggested the college group of the church plant they had been attending. The college pastor happened to be a staff member with InterVarsity Christian Fellowship. He invited me to come to a week-long camp in the Upper Peninsula with him and a bunch of other students. As a Yooper (someone from the Upper Peninsula, or UP), I was itching to get back near home, and I knew my spiritual life was in shambles. I remember seeing all the excited students and feeling dread gather in my stomach. *If they only knew the things I've done they'd send me right back home*, I thought. Yet that week, between making friends with other students, spending time in Scripture and canoeing in the vibrant waters of Lake Huron, the Lord gently spoke to me and began to heal me of the shame I'd felt over my choices.

One night after listening to a Bible exposition, I was walking back to the lodge. I looked up at the endless, dark sky scattered with vibrant stars. I sensed Jesus saying to me, "Jessica, I want your whole life. Not just part of it. Will you follow me as your Lord? I don't just want to save your soul, I want to lead every area of your life—your dreams, your fears, your relationships and finances. Everything. Will you follow me?" It was a quiet moment of surrender that unleashed a flood of joy and purpose into my life. Driving back to Michigan State at the end of the week, I was bursting with excitement and declared, "I want to tell all of Michigan State about Jesus!!"

Back on campus I got involved in the InterVarsity chapter and bumbled through what it meant to actually follow Jesus in everyday life. My Lordship decision, as I called it, seemed to spark a lot of questions: Was Jesus really the only way to God? Could I still drink but not get drunk at the keg parties? Could I still wear silver vinyl pants or was there something sinful about that? Did I have to read the Bible every day? Could I trust God to provide a job if I switched my major from turf-grass management to English? I had a community that helped me figure out those things, and a great Inter-Varsity staff worker named Joe who prayed with me and laughed with me in all of these questions. He loved me for who I was and patiently answered my questions to the best of his ability.

After college Joe invited me to volunteer with InterVarsity at retreats and conferences even though I was determined I'd go to law school, make a pile of money and save the earth through environmental law. That summer, Joe invited a bunch of graduating seniors on a road trip to Ithaca, New York, where his family still lived and where he had attended college at Cornell University. On the way there we were listening to my road-trip mix tape of the Red Hot Chili Peppers, Gangstarr, the Beastie Boys, and Peter, Paul and Mary. Joe casually said, "I think you and my brother Dave would really hit it off. You guys have similar tastes in things."

Over the next few months Dave and I did hit it off. I also grew to love helping college students explore their big questions in life and what Jesus had to say about them. I started to really dig Dave. He and I would send endless emails to each other while I worked at a law firm and he finished up his last year at Cornell. We'd refill our calling cards and have conversations that stretched on for hours. We'd talk about pop culture, theology, what we struggled with and what we dreamed about, being simultaneously serious and silly together.

That fall Joe invited me to a prospective staff retreat with Inter-Varsity, and as we were driving home I sensed that God was calling me to join the staff of InterVarsity. As I was processing these things with Joe, I also shared about my growing relationship with his brother Dave. Joe grinned wildly and jested, "What if you guys got married? That would be hilarious!" It was hilarious. Because seven months later we were engaged. Joe is a master recruiter—recruiting me to join InterVarsity staff and to marry his brother all in a matter of months.

Being married to Dave has been one of the primary ways God has helped me to follow him. As our pastor described in marriage counseling, "Your spouse is like a velvet hammer that God uses to shape and mold you into more of his likeness—it is simultaneously tough and tender." Though we both thought the analogy was supremely cheesy and at times would shout out "Velvet hammer!" to each other when we got in a fight, the analogy has been so true. Dave helps me to remember what following Jesus is all about—a love relationship lived out in community with a God who endlessly extends grace to us.

Once when I was freaked out about how much I needed to teach my students in a Bible study, he pointedly asked me, "Jess, what does a person need to do to be saved?"

I began to rattle off a list: "Well, you need to care about the poor, and tithe, and read Scripture to learn about how the Lord wants you to live, and care about global missions . . ." The list went on for a while.

Dave patiently listened to me and finally said, "All those things are good. But Jesus says all you need to do to be saved is to confess and believe that he is Lord."

I stared back at him, wondering how I could have forgotten that essential truth. Even as a "professional minister," I found myself inching further and further away from what it meant to follow Jesus into mission. I had begun to make following him about doing stuff rather than being with him. Over the years Dave and I have both encouraged each other to remember what life with Jesus is about—confessing and believing he is Lord, and inviting others to do the same. Now we get to do the same thing with our two sons, Reuben and Oswald. And God uses them as well to remind us that life with Jesus is about experiencing his love for us and extending his love to others.

This isn't a spectacularly dramatic story. I grew up in a Christian home, made a decision to follow Jesus in college, got married to a wonderful man, had some awesome kids, and we're trying to live out our faith together. Sounds pretty lame when I say it like that, right? I can remember as a middle schooler at church camp hearing a shocking testimony from another girl about her teen pregnancy and overcoming addictions. Though I should have marveled at God's grace to her, all I could think was, "Man. My testimony really sucks. It's so boring." When we compare our stories to others' it's a losing game. The point isn't what kind of a story we've lived, but that God has broken into our world to give each of us a story of how we were lost and then he found us.

> When we compare our stories to others' it's a losing game.

Not everyone has a sensational salvation story, but the point is that God can make his story true in each of our lives. We need to recognize and communicate those stories no matter how spectacular or ordinary they are because Jesus is unfolding his love and grace to us every day.

How About You?

Can you relate to my story? Maybe you've felt at a loss because nothing dramatic has happened in your life to make a good story about Jesus entering your world. Perhaps your story is incredibly dramatic and you've found that people are so shocked by how God has met you that they aren't sure how to respond for themselves to begin to follow Jesus.

Wherever you are, you can begin by asking, How is my life different today because of Jesus? How am I relating to people differently because of Jesus? How have my priorities changed? How has Jesus affected the way I spend my time, money or resources? What has shifted inside of me because of the Holy Spirit's dwelling inside of me?

People love to take "before" pictures of themselves when they're starting a weight-loss program or skin-care regimen to visually see how much weight they've lost or how their skin is clearer. If you took a "before" shot of your soul as you stepped out to share Jesus, what would it look like? Would it be a cloudy picture of fear, apathy, indifference and resentment? What if Jesus wants to transform your soul into a vibrant dwelling of the Holy Spirit filled with joy, hope and love that spills out into every interaction you have?

Taking Time to Reflect

It takes a little while to reflect on these things, but being able to share your story with others paints a picture of what life with Jesus could be like for them. Life with Jesus isn't meant to be an abstract reality of Bible-verse memory, church attendance or vague platitudes we hang on plaques on our walls to show we're Christians. Life with Jesus is meant to be different from life on our own. If it isn't, you might want to ask yourself why. One way to begin exploring your story is to ask yourself some questions: *How is my day different today because of Jesus? In what areas of my life am I being challenged to trust Jesus and submit to his leadership? Where do I experience joy because of what Jesus is doing? What are things that I feel scared, angry or anxious about that I'm trying to trust Jesus with? How have I experienced the presence of God today?*

Once we're aware of how Jesus is working in our life story, we're able to communicate it to others. An easy way to build this discipline of reflection into your life is to practice an ancient discipline called examen. "The prayer of Examen is a way of assessing one's life before

God on a regular basis. This prayer was first developed by Ignatius of Loyola in *The Spiritual Exercises*. He urged all the members of his society to use this prayer daily, even when the necessities of travel, work, and ministry made other forms of prayer impossible."[2] With a few simple questions to consider at the end of the day, the examen helps us to reflect on internal and external actions, where we aligned with God and his love and where we resisted God and his love for others or ourselves. By becoming more conscious of these actions and attitudes, we become grateful, prayerfully reflecting on his grace to us. It also helps us to become more gracious toward others as we realize the ways we have failed at loving them.

Examen is a simple prayer that only takes ten to fifteen minutes and serves you in being connected with Jesus and the people in your life because you're able to tell them a story of what it has meant for you to follow Jesus. By becoming aware of how he's changing you from the inside out, you can know your story of God's unwavering love for you even when you're a big jerk to your insensitive colleague or your friend's obnoxious boyfriend.

The Unchanging Gospel

Recently, I've been challenged by the Spirit to slow down and embrace the mundane in my life as a way to love my family and trust Jesus with what he's given me. This has meant trusting him that, though my dream is to be a full-time writer and evangelistic speaker across the world, I'm being invited to wash, fold and actually put away the laundry instead of letting it sit in a pile at the foot of my bed where I have to rummage for a pair of clean underwear every day.[3]

When people have asked me how I've been, I've been sharing with them how I'm trusting God to help me love my family by caring for their needs, to have a home that's a hospitable place of peace instead of a place of chaos. It's not a big or dramatic story, but it's one people can relate to as they figure out how to manage their stuff and care for themselves and the people in their lives. Often our sharing about the small ways we're choosing to trust Jesus can be as meaningful as sharing the big, spectacular decisions that require a ton of prayer. These days my shoes aren't fancy—they're ordinary Keds and flip-flops that help me to do what I need to do each day. They're the same shoes that many of my friends and neighbors are in, and when I'm with them I talk about what trusting Jesus looks like in this context. In everyday conversation, small things come up that serve as an opportunity for us to tell others about how Jesus is influencing our choices, time and relationships.

We have a gamut of shoes in our wardrobe, ready to wear for whatever event or circumstance we have. We are the same person wherever we go, but just as our shoes change for our context, so does the way we share the gospel. The message doesn't change, but how we share it can vary. At times it will be more appropriate to pray and move slowly with a friend. At other times the Holy Spirit will invite us to take risks and boldly challenge others to follow Jesus. It's up to us to be ready with our gospel shoes to share the gospel in a variety of ways. Paul masterfully does this throughout his ministry, depending on whether he was preaching to the Jews or the Gentiles. It can look different and sound different, but still contain the essential elements: a God who loves us, our sin that separates us from him, his love for us in sending Jesus to live on earth and die on our behalf, Jesus' resurrection that enables us to love God and others and live in the power of the Holy Spirit. Anywhere we go we carry with us the gospel story; we live it out, we speak about it. The message unfolds in words and deeds, in silence and in conversation.

In the book *Introducing the Missional Church*, Alan J. Roxburgh and M. Scott Boren write,

Each of our contexts is unique; each has its own particular

intermixing of cultural interactions. The gospel, therefore, must always be understandable in the language and thought patterns of that context. . . . It is so important for churches to become skilled in listening to their own setting. Missional life emerges from the kind of listening that connects us with what God might be up to in a particular context.[4]

At times we'll need to slip on some platform shoes to stand tall and preach the gospel in front of a large audience. Like my friends Stephanie and Heidi, you may need to get comfortable wearing high heels to go salsa dancing—doing something you love while meeting people far from God. Steel-toed boots and tennis shoes enable you to work well building a house for Habitat for Humanity with friends who don't yet know Jesus. And flip-flops are great for strolling down the streets of a crowded beach town during spring break to strike up spiritual conversations with strangers looking to connect with someone.

It doesn't matter what type of shoes you wear. The most important shoes you wear are the ones Jesus has already given you. "Wear on your feet what will prepare you to tell the good news of peace" (Ephesians 6:15 NIRV).

These Boots Are Made for Walking

Some of you have been reticent to lead in evangelism for a number of reasons: fear of what others will think of you, not being invited to do so by a pastor or other spiritual leader, or being told that you don't have the gifts or abilities to do so. To that I say, "Bullhonkey."[5] Everything can and should be used missionally to help others meet Jesus. Some of you have tremendous administrative or technology gifts that could be used to help organize large-scale outreaches that would influence millions of women. Others of you have had a desire to throw parties to enable people to experience the beauty and love of the gospel while raising millions of dollars to fund relief programs for women in your city or across the world. I'm guessing that, like me, there are others of you who dream about preaching the gospel to crowds with the hope that the Holy Spirit will move in power to bring people to salvation. I have to regularly remind myself of what the Holy Spirit spoke into my life when I was feeling timid about asking to preach at a large-scale outreach: "Don't hold back."

John 1 says everything was created by, for and through Jesus, and that includes your desire to influence people for the gospel. For Jesus' sake, don't let it get buried under a pile of should-haves or could-haves. Or as my mom likes to say, "Don't should all over yourself." Women are waiting to hear about the joy, freedom and hope that comes from the gospel. And Jesus wants to do a healing work in you as well, to remind you that "For God did not give us a Spirit of fear but of power and love and self-control" (2 Timothy 1:7 NET) to do what he has called you to do. To quote the prophet Nancy Sinatra, "These boots are made for walking." Ultimately you're accountable to Jesus to use the gifts and abilities he's given you, and you will have to stand before him someday to give account for how you've used those gifts. What will it take for you to step into the roles Jesus has been calling you into, whether ordinary or spectacular? You don't need anyone's approval but his. The bigger challenge for me hasn't been a lack of opportunities; it's been the lack of courage to pursue those opportunities or to ask for them at all.

> Just like learning to walk confidently in a pair of high heels, it takes time to step into and walk out what Jesus is calling you to do.

Just like learning to walk confidently in a pair of high heels, it takes time to step into and walk out what Jesus is calling you to do. You might feel a little wobbly at first, but in no time you'll be walking with confidence by, for and through Jesus.

Respond

Where are places you feel uncomfortable sharing about your faith in Jesus? What is one small step you can take with your "gospel shoes" to speak about or demonstrate the love of Jesus to others?

Where are places you're tempted to hold back in asking for opportunities to speak about or demonstrate Jesus, to initiate a spiritual conversation with someone, to use your gifts to help others meet Jesus? Confess these areas and ask Jesus to give you the courage and love to pursue the people and things he's inviting you to pursue.

Burning Man and
the Resurrected Man

We could hear the bass thumping from the techno tunes pumped from stacks of speakers long before our RV arrived at the dusty campsite. As we slowly pulled into the festival, we were surrounded by other RVs, old-school VW buses and trucks pulling trailers loaded with "mutant vehicles" welded to look like metal snails, giant blue narwhals and neon 8-track players. Men in poofy pink tutus, top hats and combat boots greeted us as we pulled up to the Burning Man entrance. I stepped out of the RV with gold glitter swiped across my eyelids, decked out in a fringy turquoise dress in order to resemble a peacock. The desert heat swept over my face and filled my nostrils with the scent of dust.

I collected our tickets from the rickety booth covered in graffiti and stickers for punk bands from years past. One of the tutu-clad men had a group of us stand in a circle around an old, empty oxygen tank fashioned as a large bell.

"All right! For all you virgin burners, this is a rite of passage," he yelled at us over the roar of RVs pulling up to find camping space. "You are entering into the real world. Black Rock City is home. You are here to leave the default world of cubicles, stress and ordinary life behind. Shelve all of the things that you're carrying with you. You are meant to be your real self here." Handing one of us a large mallet, he instructed us to each ring the oxygen-tank bell, strike a pose and declare, "I am not a virgin anymore!" And with the clang of the bell we were officially welcomed to Burning Man.

The Omission Trip

In 2010, six of us from Wheaton Graduate School, led by our program director, Dr. Rick Richardson, embarked on an exploratory trip to the Burning Man arts festival held in the Black Rock desert of Nevada. Since 1986 Burning Man has been an annual weeklong festival at the end of August. In 2014 an estimated sixty-five thousand people from across the world attended the festival.[1] The festival is named for the celebration at the end of the week that culminates in the burning of a 150-feet-tall wooden effigy of a man. The event is described as an experiment in community, art, radical self-expression and radical self-reliance.[2] We were compelled by the idea of what it would be like for a group of evangelicals to openly share Jesus in a community where radical self-expression, participation and radical inclusion are some of the core values, and we were curious to see how the Holy Spirit had been at work among fifty thousand neopagan, seminude participants who referred to themselves as "Burners."

I wrote on my blog before we went to Burning Man,

> I've started to refer to this trip as "the omission trip" rather than a mission trip, as unconventional of a mission trip as it might be. Mission trip sounds a little too much like we're going to do something for this crew of people, when in reality all we offer is Jesus and an openness to learn from this community of people that has often been overlooked or "omitted" by the church or religious types (hence, the trip of the over-

looked or left out). We plan to go and build relationships, pray with and for and share Jesus with fellow Burners and try to understand and connect with their spiritual longings and hopefully help them to understand and experience Jesus in a new way.[3]

It was the first time I had shared the gospel with a topless woman wearing red devil horns while drinking a latte in a neo-pagan temple with a professor from California. And this was a tame experience.

One of our biggest questions during the trip was how God wanted us to share Jesus with the Burners. At Burning Man, everyone is really nice. They're nice either because they're insanely high or because they're grateful for a week to just let it all hang out. It's a community based on gifting, so Burners cook pancakes and bacon to offer to people in the morning, host yoga classes at dawn, offer haircuts and throw elaborate parties with drinks and snacks to share with anyone who walks into the camp. We knew it wouldn't cut it just to be nice Christians. We started to wonder what gift we could offer the community. What could we—six evangelicals from Vermont, the Midwest and California—offer as a genuine gift to Burners who were either looking to escape or spiritually connect?

We began to pray. We gathered in a circle and knelt on the linoleum of our RV and asked Jesus to show us what he had to offer to Burners through us. As we prayed, tears began to stream down my face as God gave me an image of thousands of Burners worshiping and celebrating not the iconic wooden man that is the symbol of Burning Man, but Jesus, the resurrected man.

As the Holy Spirit opened our hearts to join God's love for the Burners, we realized that the gift we had to offer was prayer; we could invite Burners into the presence of the living God. Though we felt nervous going into the trip without any sort of plan for how to engage people spiritually, we shouldn't have been surprised that

the Holy Spirit was also willing to be there. We need to pray and
go to the people and places where God is directing us—even if
things aren't planned as we'd like them to be or they feel nonstrategic. From the Holy Spirit's inspiration, we decided to go to
the main gathering places at Burning Man—the temple and the
marketplace—and offer to pray for festivalgoers. Scrounging a few
pieces of cardboard, some scarves and markers, we fashioned
colorful banners that stated, "Receive your spiritual blessing or
challenge." The strategy felt reminiscent of Paul in Athens, where
he wanders through the city and is "deeply troubled by all the idols
he saw everywhere" (Acts 17:16 NLT). As Paul meets people in the
city, he begins to preach to them, "I notice that you are very religious, for as I was out walking I saw your many altars, and one of
them had this inscription on it—'To the Unknown God.' You have
been worshiping him without knowing who he is, and now I wish
to tell you about him" (Acts 17:22-23 LB). We were all excited and
nervous to see what the Holy Spirit would do.

Throughout the week, the Holy Spirit often compelled us to do
unexpected things that challenged our trust in God and willingness
to share Jesus. My friend Nicole and I talked about wanting to
boldly share our faith with others as the Holy Spirit prompted us
rather than trying to conjure up some profound experience ourselves. Just like other Burners, we wished to experience authentic,
radical self-expression through Jesus.

Wish granted. And then some.

Nicole is a bohemian amazon who is stunningly gorgeous. She
drops phrases casually into conversation like, "When I was a professional face painter . . ." or, "The seventeenth triathlon I did . . ."
She's also the kind of person who just starts popping and locking
at a hip-hop dance party because somewhere along the line she
learned how to groove like that. Nicole's coolness factor seemed to
triple in my mind each day we were there. By the end of the week,

I even saw people emulate her style of makeup because she is just that noticeable and stylish. Nicole also never had a problem getting people to agree to pray with her. I only had a breakdown one of the days I was there because I felt so insecure being around her.

Toward the end of the week, Nicole attended an ecstatic dance workshop, where she began to encounter the Holy Spirit and felt led to lift her hands in worship and declare her love for Jesus among the swirling, twirling Burners who were expressing themselves through evolving movement. As you can imagine, Nicole was nervous to start yelling about her love for Jesus, but having the indwelling presence of the Holy Spirit is a little like a spiritual laxative: you really can't hold it in. She obeyed and started saying at the top of her lungs with hands raised to the sky, "Holy! Holy! Holy! Jesus, you are love!"

After the workshop ended, a woman beelined toward Nicole.

"Were you the one talking about Jesus?" she asked. "I feel like Jesus has been after me for a while and I'm not quite sure what to do. By the way, I'm Dana."

Not only was Nicole surprised, but she was also thrilled that her willingness to take a risk meant that she could connect with someone who was curious about Jesus. As they sat down on colorful pillows strewn around the edge of the bright, billowing tent, Dana began to share with Nicole about her unconventional spiritual journey.[4]

Jesus in the Strip Club

Working as a stripper in LA, Dana began to wonder if Jesus was able to help her deal with a lot of difficult issues in her life. She began to pray and seek help from Jesus in everything, from giving her peace in her dream life to providing rent money.

"A few months ago," Dana said, "I was short $700 for my rent, which was due the next day. Sunday is a slow day at the club, and

I was really stressed out that I wouldn't make any money for my rent. Even though I had no idea how it would happen, I prayed that Jesus would provide the $700."

As Nicole was recounting this story to me, I interrupted her to ask, "How did you respond when she started to share this stuff with you?" We evangelicals don't often hear the words *prayer* and *strip club* in the same sentence.

Nicole laughed. "What could I say? I prayed that Jesus would give me an open mind and asked her to tell me more!" Though the Holy Spirit can be like a spiritual laxative, he can also be like a spiritual Tums—amazingly soothing when things start to feel crazy.

> Though the Holy Spirit can be like a spiritual laxative, he can also be like a spiritual Tums—amazingly soothing when things start to feel crazy.

Dana shared with her how God provided for her needs during her shift that Sunday. Her first customer gave her an unusually large tip. Her second customer, a regular, came in and thanked her for advice she had given him that had helped his health improve; he too gave her a huge tip as a thank-you.

"At this point, I was only $300 away from having my whole rent met!" Dana shared. "But the most amazing thing was the last guy who came in for the night; his name was Jesus!" (At this point, I was trying to imagine the look on Nicole's face as Dana told her that she had given a lap dance to a Hispanic customer named Jesus.) "Jesus gave me the last $300 I needed for my rent! It seems so clear how God was caring for me and gave me a sign that he wants to provide for me!"

Scripture reminds us that our bodies are created by God to be used for his purposes. 1 Corinthians 6:19 says, "Do you not know that your bodies are temples of the Holy Spirit, who is in you, whom you have received from God? You are not your own." While giving lap dances is outside of Scripture's instructions to honor God with one's body, I can't deny Dana's spiritual experience. As someone who wasn't yet a Jesus follower, these weren't words Dana lived by. To expect her to do so would have imposed the law of God without extending her the grace of God. This story is offensive not because Dana worked in a strip club and was experiencing Jesus' reaching out to her, but that Jesus reaches out to us regardless of who we are or where we are. He loves strippers and religious churchgoers exactly the same. There is nothing we can do to earn his love or forgiveness—he gives it to each of us as a gift.

As they prayed together and exchanged contact information, Nicole encouraged Dana to keep looking out for how Jesus (the Son of God, not the lap-dance customer) was pursuing her. I'm thankful that during their bizarre interaction the Holy Spirit was able to guide Nicole into loving Dana just where she was, to help her see that Jesus was searching for her, that he loved her and could even meet her at Burning Man. Since then, Dana has connected with other Christians and, God willing, is continuing to experience Jesus in both personal and unexpected ways.

Anyone, Anywhere

It didn't make a lot of sense for us to go to Burning Man, a place most evangelicals would label evil, scandalous or closed to the gospel. A friend decided to watch a documentary about Burning Man after hearing that Dave and I had attended the festival a few years ago. Though my friend had enjoyed the party scene and is very open-minded, when she told me about the documentary, she declared with wide eyes, "I really couldn't picture you guys there—it sounds like such a crazy place." It is a crazy place. But Dana's story reminded me just how often we forget that Jesus can reach anyone he wants to, wherever he wants to.

As Christians, we can wrongly assume that the only place Jesus hangs out is in churches, Bible studies or organized mission trips. Though we may not realize it, he takes us to places every day with marginalized people who need to experience his love. I once heard a preacher describe the Holy Spirit as "promiscuous." Though that is typically a negative term, I thought it was the perfect descriptor for the wild and boundless person of the Trinity who will love on anyone, anywhere to help them meet Jesus.

The six of us from Wheaton weren't the only ones called into the desert to share Jesus. In Acts 8, the church is persecuted and scattered, beginning the fulfillment of Jesus' words in Acts 1:8, "You will be my witnesses in Jerusalem, and in all Judea and Samaria, and to the ends of the earth." Philip, one of the members of the church, went to Samaria to see how the Holy Spirit had been at work. At that time, going to Samaria was a little like going to Burning Man as an evangelical Christian. Samaritans would have been suspicious of Philip—a Jew from Jerusalem—and wondered if he had come to judge and look down on them. Culturally, Jews weren't even supposed to associate with Samaritans because they were deemed unclean. Philip had no plan. He had no idea where his friends were—if they were dead, in prison or if they had moved to the next town over. Philip could have cowered in fear, hidden out in someone's home until things cooled down or began to question whether following Jesus was worth his life. But he didn't. Instead, he began to go to cities that most Jews would have never set foot in. If he had told them before he went, most people would have responded, "You're going where? To Samaria? What if some of the evil or sin gets on you? Are you sure it's safe?" It wasn't safe.

But as Philip crossed cultural and ethnic barriers and proclaimed Jesus, people were healed, they listened with curiosity about Jesus, and Scripture says, "there was great joy in that city" (Acts 8:8). God gave Philip a thriving ministry among people who welcomed and responded to his preaching. He could have stayed there to form a large church, trained many more to preach the gospel and have his fame grow through the signs and healings he was performing. He could have built a megachurch. How much of Philip's ego was on the line when the Lord had a change of plans for his ministry?

An angel appeared to Philip and instructed him to go to the desert. It is bizarre for Scripture to say, "Now an angel of the Lord said to Philip. . . ." (Acts 8:26) without any description of Philip's emotional reaction or what he had been doing when the angel showed up. Was he praying silently and an angel descended to speak to him? Was he helping himself to another bowl of lentil soup when a towering figure in white appeared suddenly? Was he kneeling in prayer, worshiping Jesus? We find a clue in Philip's response as to why God saw fit to send an angel to talk to him: Philip listened for the promptings of God and was humble and obedient to follow the Holy Spirit. The instructions from the Spirit were more important than his agenda or his existing ministry.

Though there was no explanation of why he should leave a growing ministry or what he would do once he got to the desert road, Philip took off. His response shows how being formed by Jesus in solitude cultivates obedience and attentiveness to the Holy Spirit, even to the most seemingly outlandish requests. It wasn't strategic for Philip to leave a thriving ministry in Samaria and go solo into the desert. But because Philip was confident that following Jesus' plans was better than following his own plans, he went.[5]

> Being formed by Jesus in solitude cultivates obedience and attentiveness to the Holy Spirit, even to the most seemingly outlandish requests.

I'm not sure I would have been as obedient as Philip. I'm a big fan of strategy. I like waking up each day with a plan of what I'm going to do and how I'm going to do it. However, I'm also a big fan of spontaneity and pushing the envelope. That's why, when Dr. Richardson began to talk about what it would be like for a group of evangelicals to go to Burning Man to share Jesus, I was intrigued. Though I didn't have an angel appear to me, I had a sense it was a place God wanted me to go. And I have to admit that I loved seeing jaws drop and eyes bug out when I told Christian friends that I was going to Burning Man with a group from Wheaton College Graduate School. I liked reminding people that Jesus invites us to do crazy things with people with whom few are willing to spend time.

While strolling through the desert, Philip saw a chariot carrying an Ethiopian eunuch, a high government official traveling back to Ethiopia from Jerusalem. Though the eunuch had wealth and power, he was an outcast. He had gone to Jerusalem to worship and learn about God, but he would have been prohibited from even entering the temple because of his ethnicity and castration. Though he was someone with whom few Jewish people would have made an effort to talk, Philip ran up to his chariot and heard the eunuch reading the book of Isaiah aloud.

Philip asked, "Do you understand what you are reading?"

"How can I unless someone explains it to me?" the eunuch responded.

So he invited Philip to sit with him in his chariot, bumping along a dusty desert road to learn about Jesus the Messiah. During this interaction Philip put aside what might make him uncomfortable—the eunuch's wealth, status, ethnicity and physical deformity—to share Jesus. The Holy Spirit had been working in the desert all along; Philip simply had to be obedient to follow Jesus to an unlikely place to care for a marginalized person seeking God.

Luke, the author of Acts, wrote that the eunuch saw water and asked to be baptized as a sign of his willingness to follow Jesus. The eunuch became the first missionary to Africa, and the Ethiopian Orthodox Church traces its roots to the evangelization of this eunuch. In contrast to how Christianity spread in the Greco-

Roman world through the lower class, Christianity came through the royal courts in Ethiopia because of this eunuch.[6] What could have been deemed a nonstrategic, irresponsible, crazy jaunt to the desert was an adventure in following the Holy Spirit to a seemingly outlandish place to proclaim Jesus to a marginalized person. Though there were likely thousands benefiting from Philip's ministry, the Holy Spirit had more concern for one God-seeking eunuch who was waiting for someone to enter his world and share Jesus.

The Ethiopian eunuch never saw Philip again after he was baptized. Philip did all he could to prepare him to follow Jesus during this brief interaction. Yet the whole continent of Africa was influenced because of the presence and power of Jesus in the Ethiopian eunuch's life. Nicole could only stay involved in Dana's life to the extent she was able. She couldn't meet with her for three years, let alone three weeks to disciple her. But she did what she could to help Dana continue to meet Jesus and be part of a community that would help her to do so. Then she trusted the Holy Spirit to prompt other people to care for Dana as well. We are not in control of what happens from the seeds of the gospel we scatter. God is. It's a mystery, yet we can choose to love, take risks and be faithful to wherever and whomever the Spirit leads us, no matter how long or short that time might be.

> We are not in control of what happens from the seeds of the gospel we scatter. God is.

Just Go

It can be far too easy to dismiss the people and places that have been omitted by the church as too scary, too sinful, too evil. Our egos, strategies and fears can get in the way of obeying the Holy Spirit's directions to go. While men might struggle with wanting to build their own kingdoms and seem important, women struggle with stepping out to be different or fearing making a mistake. On either side it's pride—pride that we can create the kingdom of God ourselves or fear that the small things we do are enough to topple God's plans.

Because women are relationally focused, we can justify that if we don't have a long-term strategy for discipleship after someone becomes a Christian, we shouldn't take any risks at all. Jesus instructs us to make disciples, not converts. But we place too much emphasis on ourselves when we believe that evangelism is entirely up to us, or that God can't use us at all. Regardless of how you feel, Jesus is alive and working in these places to let people know that he loves them. We need to prayerfully discern how God is directing us and obey him however long or short that process of discipleship, and regardless of how it makes us feel.

At Burning Man, Nicole exchanged information with Dana and kept in touch with her as much as she could, emailing her and praying for her regularly. A few months after Burning Man, my husband and I were at an InterVarsity staff conference sharing about our experiences in the desert, and we shared the Dana story. After our talk a surfer-dude staff member from San Diego raised his hand and said, "Dana actually stayed at our house for two weeks. Nicole got in touch with us and connected us with her since she knew there was InterVarsity in California. She and my wife prayed and studied Scripture together while she lived with us, because she needed a place to crash before moving back to Australia. We had a lot of crazy late-night talks with her. We're still praying for her." My husband and I were happily stunned at the sovereignty of God when his people willingly take risks.

We just don't know what will happen. But we do know God is sovereign and wants to see the whole world lovingly bow in worship before him. Like Dana the stripper and the Ethiopian eunuch, there are people waiting for someone to enter their world who is willing to share what it means to follow Jesus. God loves his people and sends his Holy Spirit to continue to woo people to himself no matter how involved we are able to be in their lives. Jesus is able to use even small interactions with people to change the rest of their lives. Our responsibility is to prayerfully risk, to love people in word and deed, and to go where they are. Sometimes that's across the street to a neighbor's home, other times it is to a new city or country to follow Jesus. Each day, he invites us to be present with the people in our lives and to whatever way we can share Jesus with them. Do we have the courage to go?

Response

Who are people in your life you frequently find yourself thinking about or praying for? Who are people that scare you? Who are people you feel a natural affinity toward?

Pray that God would give you the courage to follow the Holy Spirit to people and places that might make you feel uncomfortable. Pray that you would have the faith to follow where he leads.

Connecting God's Story,
My Story & Her Story

In *Reimagining Evangelism*, Dr. Rick Richardson (of Burning Man fame) writes, "Stories are a bigger and better container for the whole of the truth than propositions, concepts and dogmas. . . . When our truth is enfleshed in . . . stories, . . . people are interested. . . . We must recover our own stories, and God's Big Story, and connect them to the stories of people we love and are reaching out to."[1] Richardson points to three important dynamics in evangelism: becoming familiar with our own story, becoming familiar with the story of God in Scripture and being able to connect them to others. Stories are powerful tools that can help us be more effective in sharing the gospel. It takes time to reflect, and fortunately there are movies and preachers and writers out there who help us get in touch with our own stories of heartbreak, loss, victory and shame.

> Stories are powerful tools that can help us be more effective in sharing the gospel.

In college, I saw the 1998 German thriller *Run, Lola, Run*, a story about Lola, who needs to procure $100,000 in twenty minutes to save her boyfriend's life. The movie is shot in three different scenarios, all beginning the same way but ending differently. In each of the runs,

Lola's interactions with people affect them in diffe
times positively, sometimes negatively. The film ex]
free will versus determinism, cause and effect, a
theory—how incidental encounters and choices can untold into
much larger effects. It explores religious and philosophical ideas
without being a "religious" movie.

Walking back to my apartment after the film, I was awestruck
seeing the embodiment of a huge theological concept played out
so brilliantly on the screen. It made me examine my own choices
and beliefs about how I interacted with others and what that meant
for my spiritual life. I breathlessly exclaimed to my roommates,
"Wow, Americans should make more movies like that. That was
way better than anything I've ever seen!" To which they chided me
with their opinions on what incredible movies *The Wedding Singer*,
Saving Private Ryan and *Ever After* were. To their credit, *The Big
Lebowski*, directed by the Coen brothers, and Wes Anderson's
Rushmore came out in the same year, so there was some pretty epic
cinematography going on in the United States in 1998.

Over the years I've found that I've been able to weave God's
story, my story and the story of the person I'm talking to in a way
that's both relevant to them and theologically sound. Figure 7.1
demonstrates this.

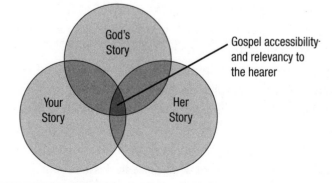

Figure 7.1

Stories stay with us and shape our worldview. Christine Dillon, author of *Telling the Gospel Through Story*, writes,

> In contrast to a sermon, where a listener tends to stand "outside" and "look in" on what the preacher is saying, stories draw people into the heart of the narrative. Without even realizing it they begin to see the stories as real. Whenever people tell me they don't believe the Bible, I always respond, "That's fine, just listen to the story." They almost never mention their unbelief again. Somewhere along the way, they're drawn into the reality of the Bible. It's been a long time since I've had to use apologetics in response to the request to "prove to me that the Bible is true."[2]

As a church planter, Dillon has shared the gospel across the world with people of many different faith backgrounds. It's the story of God that draws in her listeners regardless of what they believe. The gospel is an embodied message. It's embodied in Jesus and it's embodied in his followers in Scripture and in the world today. It's embodied in you, and in your story.

> The gospel is an embodied message. . . . It's embodied in you, and in your story.

God's Story: The Gospel

When I took a class on evangelistic preaching from Dr. Lon Allison during graduate school, he shared a helpful way to think about communicating the embodied gospel. There are many God stories throughout Scripture that illustrate how God desires to interact with his people, but there is only one gospel. For an increasingly biblically illiterate culture, many of the stories we Christians share—from Adam and Eve, to Moses and the Ten Commandments, to Jesus dying on the cross—are completely unfamiliar. People have a vague idea of what these stories are about, likely from pop culture or from stories they heard as children.

Figure 7.2

It is essential to know the gospel message and be able to communicate it verbally. When I was beginning to share my faith I would study gospel outlines such as the bridge diagram and practice sharing them with my husband. I wanted to make sure that I could communicate the essential truth of Scripture and to know it for myself. Any basic gospel outline should include God's love for us, our separation from God because of our sin, Jesus' ability to save us through his death on the cross, and his resurrection, which gives us power to live each day.

In recent years I've enjoyed using James Choung's Big Story gospel outline from his book *True Story* because it not only focuses on personal salvation, but also includes how God wants to restore the whole world.[3] You can find ways to access the Big Story gospel outline in Appendix A. Take time to learn it and practice sharing it with someone else—you can even share it with someone who isn't a Christian and ask them what they think of it! Know the gospel. This is the first and most important part of evangelism. The gospel is simple, profound and succinct—the essence of Scripture boiled down for anyone to understand and access it.

Your Story and God's Story: Make It Human

Sharing the gospel as a theological concept will help people begin to understand the truths of what Scripture says, but it won't necessarily help them know what it means for their lives. In a relativistic culture, the nonembodied gospel is simply another set of beliefs amid many others. I can remember sharing the gospel with a guy on a college campus in West Virginia, outlining the truths about God's love for us, our sin, Jesus' ability to save us from our sin and his resurrection to give us new life.

"That's really interesting," he responded. "I learned a lot of new stuff from you about the Bible! Thanks for talking with me today!" Though our interaction was positive, I couldn't figure out how to steer the conversation toward how the gospel applied to *him*, and I felt frustrated and discouraged. This wasn't just meant to be an abstract theology I subscribed to; it was meant to be an invitation for him to make the story true in his own life. Wasn't it enough to simply get the gospel out there?

At other times I've tried to focus on sharing my own story, helping people to see what life with Jesus could be like and what it's meant to me. Testimonies are powerful ways for others to see evidence of the work of Christ in a person's life. However, we don't want people to simply be encouraged or challenged by our stories; we want them to begin to see how Jesus wants to heal them from the inside out too!

Figure 7.3 illustrates connecting God's story and your story—connecting the gospel with personal life change. A story of personal life change could be as simple as how you've begun to pray on your morning commute instead of mentally rehearsing the details of the arguments you've been having with your colleague. It could be a story of emotional or physical healing, of how Jesus has changed the ways you think, act and feel as you have trusted him with various areas of your life. It doesn't need to be your whole story and it doesn't need to be a dramatic story. The point of stories isn't how awesome they are; the point is that God is awesome! And he takes each of us in our context and makes something new as we repent, turning from ourselves as lord and confessing and believing that Jesus is Lord.

The word *testimony* conjures up a specific idea of what type of story needs to be shared. Beau Crosetto, in his book *Beyond Awkward*, has a great section on writing your Lordship/Transformational story, which involves taking aspects of your life and being able to describe how Jesus has influenced them.[4] It can be more

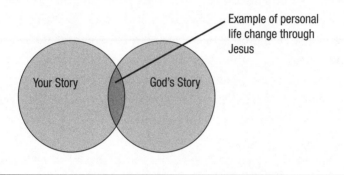

Figure 7.3

beneficial to others to tell your story thematically as opposed to chronologically. A friend who struggles with depression may not care how you prayed a sinner's prayer at church camp when you were ten years old, but I'm guessing that he or she would be curious how you have found comfort in the Psalms to know that God loves you even when you feel depressed.

Your Story and Her Story: Empathetic Listening

As the Big Story gospel outline illustrates, God is about more than just saving our souls. He is on a mission to bring heaven to earth. We want people to see that God cares about injustice, poverty, racism and corruption, but that he also cares about them. He wants to heal us from the inside out to become agents of healing in our world.

While training some student and staff evangelists at a large university during an outreach focusing on anti-human-trafficking efforts, I overheard a student named Sharita sharing vulnerably about her struggle to forgive the man who had sexually abused her as a child. Lydia, the staff member who was talking with her, was amazingly empathetic and shared her own story about forgiveness and Jesus' ability to help us love our enemies. It was profound that as she entered into discussion about Jesus' power to heal on a macrolevel to combat modern-day slavery, it became applicable to her personal suffering on a microlevel. Near the end of the conversation they were both in tears and gave each other a hug, though many students were passing through the union on their way to class. Sharita thanked Lydia for sharing her story with her while she wrote down her contact information for the InterVarsity chapter to stay in touch with her.

Afterward I asked Lydia how the conversation had gone from her perspective. "Good!" She replied, wiping her eyes with a tissue. "Sharita and I really connected, and I can't believe how she opened up about such painful areas in her life."

"How did she respond to the gospel?" I asked, curious about how she was able to weave the story of God into her own story and Sharita's story. "It seems like God was really moving in the conversation!"

"That's what I was trying to figure out," said Lydia. "She and I connected really well, there was a ton of empathy, but it was hard to transition into what the gospel meant for her and to invite her to respond to Jesus. I wanted there to be more than just a connection with each other. I wanted her to connect to God!"

Though Lydia was frustrated, her conversation with Sharita highlights an important way for women to share Jesus with each other. In *The Athena Doctrine: How Women (and the Men Who Think Like Them) Will Rule the Future*, authors John Gerzema and Michael D'Antonio explore feminine leadership qualities and the assets they are to leadership and business. They write, "Empathy is the starting point for exploring social needs and building a closer connection with your customer."[5] Later they write, "Vulnerability is today the most important agent of change management."[6] We aren't trying to sell Jesus—he is a person, not a product. When people act like that, evangelism gets forced and creepy. But empathy goes a long way in helping people to see that they are cared for by God and by his people.

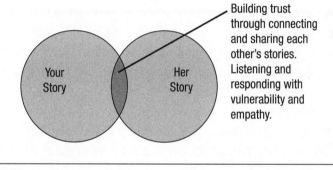

Building trust through connecting and sharing each other's stories. Listening and responding with vulnerability and empathy.

Your Story

Her Story

Figure 7.4

The concept of empathy as a catalyst for change and vulnerability as a change agent is seen throughout Scripture. Jesus and his followers take the time to listen to and empathize with the people they meet, even in brief encounters. Often we're caught off guard when people are vulnerable, and in those moments we can ignore what they have shared or take the opportunity to respond with empathy and demonstrate the love of Jesus.

At a wedding I had just officiated for a close friend, I was enjoying the reception and chatting with a gay couple while we ate wedding cake. After sharing that I was a campus minister, Corey, one of the men, said, "Yeah, I was involved in a Christian campus group when I was in college." His frustrated tone hinted that it hadn't been a positive experience, so I asked him more about it.

"They basically ran me out of the group when I confessed I was gay," he said, looking me in the eyes, clearly wondering how I would respond as a Christian minister.

I looked back at him. "I'm so sorry, Corey. That should never have happened. Jesus loves you and I'm really sorry that you were treated that way. It breaks my heart when I hear stories like this."

Corey's face brightened. I'm not sure he expected an apology from someone he could have lumped in with the intolerant Christians on his campus.

"It's no big deal," he said as he poked at the frosting on his cake. "It just sort of messed me up with the whole God thing for a while. By the way, do you do gay weddings?" His partner shot him a look of mock surprise as I started laughing and said that I had just done this one wedding as a kindness to my friend Tara.

Corey's confession could have caught me off guard. I wasn't expecting to have a conversation like this at a wedding reception. I could have shrugged off his comment by minimizing his pain, saying, "Yeah, sadly some Christians are like that." However, because of years of listening to the Holy Spirit and Jesus teaching me to empathize rather than ignore, I was ready to engage him emotionally. One of the first fruits of the conversion process is often confession. This shouldn't surprise us because as Jesus begins to illuminate the dark places of the heart, the Holy Spirit prompts us to confess these areas of brokenness to God and to one another. As Jesus heals us from the inside out, the indwelling of his Holy Spirit compels us to surrender areas of pain and brokenness.

For Corey, God seemed to be opening his heart to recognize one of the barriers to following Jesus: Christians had hurt him and poorly represented Jesus to him. Our stories connected. Confession takes place all along the conversion process, but can especially be seen as the Holy Spirit knocks down walls put up to protect broken hearts.

The God of Empathy

In Luke 8:42-48 Jesus demonstrates empathy to a woman who has been suffering from perpetual bleeding.

> As Jesus was on his way, the crowds almost crushed him. And a woman was there who had been subject to bleeding for twelve years, but no one could heal her. She came up behind him and touched the edge of his cloak, and immediately her bleeding stopped.
>
> "Who touched me?" Jesus asked.
>
> When they all denied it, Peter said, "Master, the people are crowding and pressing against you."
>
> But Jesus said, "Someone touched me; I know that power has gone out from me."
>
> Then the woman, seeing that she could not go unnoticed, came trembling and fell at his feet. In the presence of all the people, she told why she had touched him and how she had been instantly healed. Then he said to her, "Daughter, your faith has healed you. Go in peace."

Because of the laws of purity in Jewish culture (see Leviticus 15:19-33), this woman is unable to worship at the temple because she is considered unclean. Anyone who comes into contact with her is also deemed unclean. The medical help she has received has only made her condition worse and she has been driven into poverty trying to get additional help. The physical pain, loneliness, shame and social isolation the woman must feel are tremendous. InterVarsity Press's *Women's Bible Commentary* states,

> Jesus' concern is not for the woman's impurity but for her faith. He shows no repugnance for the bodily function that is a recurrent feature of all women's experience. In contrast to Mark's account, in which the woman speaks privately to Jesus

(Mk 5:33), Jesus asks her to make a public confession. While this might seem to expose her to embarrassment, her condition could scarcely have remained a secret for twelve years; and the declaration along with Jesus' affirmation marks the definitive end of her devastating affliction and her reentry into human society as an acceptable person.[7]

In her sermon "Encounters with Jesus from Dying to Life," noted African American civil rights leader and preacher Prathia L. Hall further illustrates what it was like for this woman.

> Imagine this poor woman's condition—365 days of checking for stains, worrying about overflow, and planning what she would wear based on what was happening in her body. . . .
>
> Twelve years times twelve months of light-headed weakness. Twelve years times twelve months of fabricating adequate sanitary protection first-century style. Twelve years times twelve months of raging hormones. Twelve years times twelve months of suffering. . . .
>
> For twelve long years life has been draining from her body, drop by drop by drop.[8]

When the woman with perpetual bleeding touches the garment of Jesus, he stops in his tracks because he empathizes with her pain. Though the crowds are pressing in around him and he is on his way to see an important official whose daughter is dying, he demonstrates that the women who are marginalized in society are important in the kingdom of God. Jesus affirms her as "Daughter," indicating full inclusion into the family of God. The woman gets her body back, but she also is granted acceptance back into society.

We see the affirmation of this woman as daughter when Jesus heals her as an individual. But the gospel's power extends far beyond us as individuals into our communities and governments. Reading this same passage in South Africa,

> Zulu women were asked to respond to [the story of the woman with perpetual bleeding] in Mark's Gospel . . . and readers strongly identified with the healed woman. They found Jesus' flouting of blood taboos all the more relevant since the local independent churches maintain such negative attitudes to menstruation. Gikuyu women immediately identified with the woman with the issue of blood, whose condition was "very real to the women who developed problems as a result of female circumcision." These readers noted "the attention and care that Jesus gave to women who were in oppressive and desperate situations."[9]

In response to these discussions of Scripture, Christian women founded a guild "to defend their own daughters against female circumcision." Philip Jenkins writes, "To understand the radical nature of this step, we have to recall the central importance of circumcision for defining femininity, sexual morality, and adulthood. This was in short a biblically fuelled social revolution."[10] The Gikuyu women saw not only that Jesus wanted to heal them, but also that he wanted to use them to redefine femininity and protect their daughters. The gospel transformed how they saw themselves and compelled them to respond to the societal oppression of female circumcision on behalf of other women. Jesus heals us through his gospel message, gives us the courage to live differently from damaging societal norms and compels us to help others who are oppressed.

For Sharita and the woman with perpetual bleeding, empathy played a key role in connecting each of these women to God and acknowledging their pain. For many people who have been hurt by the church, empathy is a primary way for Jesus to be demonstrated.

Vulnerability begets vulnerability. Women hide in shame of being "unclean" because of incest, divorce, miscarriage or depression. They hide in shame because of same-sex attraction and fear of being ostracized by their churches and communities. What a gift for someone to acknowledge their pain, to listen and vulnerably open up to say, "You aren't alone." This gift connects the story of a loving God to their story.

Your Story, Her Story and God's Story: "Real" Evangelism

Lydia was frustrated that Sharita didn't pray a sinner's prayer or confess Jesus as Lord. It didn't feel like "real" evangelism to her. The woman with perpetual bleeding experienced physical healing, and Jesus calls her "Daughter." How could these interactions be quantified? How do you measure when someone is able to forgive an enemy? When they experience emotional or physical healing? These interactions are part of the mysterious, wonderful work of evangelism—we get to join God in his work to love others. As we share Jesus we must also listen to how God is speaking to us through Scripture and become aware of how he's speaking to others individually and culturally.

One of the ways we can embrace empathy as a catalyst is to simply listen. It's a rare thing today to have someone stop and listen rather than jump in with a similar story or an attempt to one-up the other person with a similar experience. It's not convenient or efficient to sit with a grieving friend. It's difficult to listen and be present to people in grief, suffering or anxiety instead of trying to fix them or the problem they're facing. It is scary to keep our mouths shut and believe that God can speak through Scripture to both personal pain and societal injustice. We die to ourselves when we choose to empathize. We show people that they are valued, not because of what they can do, how they present themselves or what they can provide, but because they are children of God. Stopping to empathize, keeping our mouths shut and showing up even when it feels inconvenient or uncomfortable is a radical way we demonstrate Jesus to people who feel overlooked and weak. We don't need to stop with empathy and vulnerability as a way to connect with another woman, though this is a critical part of sharing Christ with her. We can help to connect God's story, our story and her story so that Jesus is able to say to her, "Daughter, your faith has made you well, go in peace."

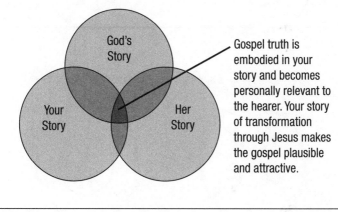

Figure 7.5

When these three things come together it demonstrates the power of God through the gospel, it helps her connect to you and hear stories about how Jesus has been real in your own life, and it opens her eyes to the possibility of what her life could be like with Jesus and the relevancy of the gospel to her.

Preaching at a chapel service in a small Christian college in Michigan, I shared my own story while demonstrating how to use the Big Story app. You can watch the full version of the message titled "Why the Gospel Is Good News for You" online.[11] My message that day illustrated how to connect God's story, your story and your hearer's story. Though I preached the message to numerous students, I use the same format when I'm sharing with an individual. The difference is that it becomes a conversation instead of a sermon.

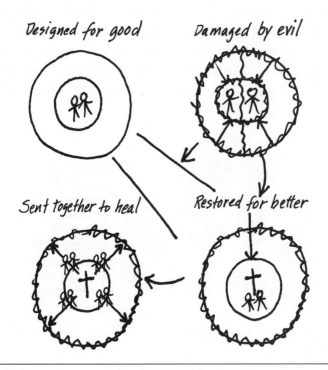

Figure 7.6

Walking Through the Big Story

Questions are crucial to building trust in evangelism. We need to engage in a dialogue with people rather than a monologue about Jesus. Questions help to take the focus off of you and what you want to share and shift the emphasis to what you really want to know anyway: "Where are you at with God?" If you've posed a question, it makes sense for you to share as well. Like in a normal conversation when you ask, "What kind of books do you enjoy?" the person shares his or her thoughts about books, and then you share yours. Below are questions I typically ask while walking through the Big Story.

1. Need for Change: "What has been something you've tried to change about your life or relationships?" "How has it been to try and change it?" "What are ways you've tried to change it?" I often share about relatable areas of life—trying to stick with a fitness routine, becoming more patient with people, forgiving someone who has wronged me. Everyone is trying to change something about their lives. It's rare to meet a person who says, "Nope, I'm good. Totally content with every area of my life."

2. Created for Good/World 1: "What are things you enjoy in life?" This touches on how God has created the world for good and gives me insight into what they are passionate about and interested in. It also provides connection points for us to get to know each other ("You like food? I like food!"). It's also a lot easier to start with the good things in the world than the bad things!

3. Damaged by Evil/World 2: "What are things that you see in the world that make you angry, break your heart or create a sense of injustice?" Again, this gives me insight into the particular passions and interests God has given them, and I'm able to share about the things I care about. God puts desires in our hearts to want the world to be made right, and it's important to prophetically affirm those things. Once, when talking with a female student who was passionate about providing quality education for special-needs kids, I simply said to her, "Melissa, I believe that God gave you that desire and wants to use you to care for marginalized kids. God shares your concern as well for special-needs kids and wants to use you to care for them!" This made the gospel become personally relevant for her because it wasn't simply a theological concept; it was an area of brokenness in the world that God was inviting her to join him in healing.

4. Restored for Better/World 3: "How would you describe Jesus?" "What are some things you know about him?" "What's your

spiritual background?" Each of these questions provides insight
into their spiritual background—whether they've grown up in
church, their opinions about Jesus and any possible barriers
they might have in following him. This is the part where Jesus'
work on the cross is explained, including how he identified,
owned and overcame. This is where the gospel gets personal. It
isn't simply about the world's problems; it's about the problem
of sin in each of our souls. It's crucial to share how Jesus is the
only way we can be healed from our sin sickness because it's
tempting to move into the last world—Sent to Heal—without
acknowledging that we must be healed from sin first in order
to be sent to heal by God.

5. Sent to Heal/World 4: "How are you following Jesus and engaging in his mission to heal the world through his community?" This question gets at two dynamics. For people who
   consider themselves Christians, it challenges the idea that
   belief in Jesus is only a personal decision. This helps the hearer
   to think about and see that following Jesus is done in community and is an active thing. For non-Christians, the
   question is the same as in Restored for Better: "Would you
   like to become a follower of Jesus and engage in his mission
   to heal the world with his community and with the help of
   his Spirit today?" Their answer will help you to see where
   they're at spiritually—if they're ready to begin to follow Jesus
   or if they have questions and doubts they want to process
   before making a decision.

   If someone isn't ready to make a faith commitment it's okay to
ask them something like, "What kinds of things would hold you
back from following Jesus?" This is another place to express empathy with fears, doubts or insecurities. Some women and men I've
met feel like they're unworthy of God's love, are afraid how their

families will respond to their decision or fear that they won't be able to follow Jesus perfectly. Ask the Holy Spirit how to care for this person and share about your own fears and doubts as you've followed Jesus. It is such a huge decision that many people fear they won't get it right if they say yes and then aren't sure how to follow Jesus. Underscore the importance of community and that none of us are meant to follow Jesus alone—that together we learn how to love and serve him and this world.

One of the easiest things we can do to share our faith is to simply know the gospel story of what it means to follow Jesus. Regardless of how you share it, the elements of the gospel should include God's love for the world, our rejection of his love and our sin against him, Jesus' sacrifice to pay for our sin and restore our relationship with God and others, and Jesus' ability to lead us into his care for the world and our relationship with God. With any outline that I use, I read over it a couple times to familiarize myself with it, practice sharing it with my husband or another Christian, and pray that God would help me share stories about how the gospel message has been real in my own life. Sharing our own stories in the midst of the gospel helps people to see what it looks like in real life. You can identify ways you've experienced the love of God, how you've been affected by sin and brokenness or are currently struggling, how Jesus has been present in those struggles or met you in a significant way, and how Jesus has been inviting you to follow him to love the world.

Response

Check out the Big Story app online or on your smartphone (available on iTunes and Google Play). Take a moment to download it and become comfortable using it. Walk through it with a friend or family member to get a feel for what it's like to share it out loud. Reflect on the places you have experienced how the world has been created for good, damaged by evil, restored for better and sent to heal. It's fine if you don't have a neat package to tie up your story. We are all in the process of living out faith in Jesus, and it's important to help people see that you're imperfect and that you still sin and make mistakes. Set up a date with a non-Christian friend and ask them if you can share the basic message of Christianity by walking through the app with them. Find more resources for using the Big Story gospel outline in Appendix A.

Experiments in Loving Others

If you ask me at any given moment, "What's on your mind?" I will likely respond with a swirl of ideas of *big* things I could do to help others meet Jesus, live out my faith in practical ways and mobilize others to do the same thing. When I take my sons to the beach in the summer I dream about organizing beach cleanups on Lake Erie to care for my beloved Great Lakes. In the spring, seeing all the kids walk home from school, I picture our neighborhood running summer art camps for at-risk kids in the area. When I walk to CVS to pick up my prescriptions, I see abandoned storefronts and imagine Christian business owners starting bakeries that employ jobless people. (Also, then I could have delicious freshly baked blueberry scones available in my neighborhood every day.) I see moms who seem lonely and disconnected as they push their kids on the swings at the playground, and I imagine what life would be like for them if they came to my MOPS group, and what it would be like if my mom friends did the same thing. I see the dumpsters behind grocery stores and think, "How many families wouldn't have to go hungry if all the waste from grocery stores and restaurants was donated to the Cleveland Food Bank?"

The problem for me isn't the lack of ideas; the problem is discerning how Jesus wants me to use my beautiful feet to bring his good news in my relationships, community and world.[1] It's easy for me to want to do something cool for Jesus, to fix a problem I see or to get frustrated and ignore the people and problems, hoping someone else does something about it. When I spend time with Jesus, he helps me discover that I'm wired to love him and love others, and he wants to do the same in each of our lives. Sometimes loving others involves doing something effortless; other times it makes us uncomfortable and stretches us in our skills and capacity to love. Both of these dynamics are part of the paradox of how Jesus wants us to love others. He invites us to be comfortably uncomfortable in loving others—to do what we enjoy yet take risks to trust him in new ways. As we experiment in connecting with Jesus and others, he directs us in the best ways to use our beautiful feet to bring his good news.

It can feel overwhelming, confusing and immobilizing to think about the needs in our communities and world and to figure out how God wants to use us to care for others. Fortunately, being comfortably uncomfortable often starts in small ways, by taking steps of obedience to trust Jesus and love others. The challenge lies in believing that our efforts are enough to care for a lost and hurting world and that *we* are enough for God to use to love others.

Jesus and Cookies

Because my mom had become a Jesus follower in college right before she married my dad, she was eager to train up her children in the way of the Lord. When we were in elementary school she involved us in the Awana program, which met at a local Baptist church. Each week our leader, Mary, would lead us in songs, Scripture memorization and games with the help of her ventriloquist doll, Tabitha, which made me beg my mom for my own ventriloquist doll that Christmas. Because my mom loves me, she didn't tell me, "No, you weirdo, you're getting a Barbie doll like all the other eight-year-olds." Instead she found a plastic Howdy Doody ventriloquist doll. My brother, sister and I would take turns pulling the little string on his back, pretending to make him talk. At Awana each week Mary would invite children to make a decision to follow Jesus, which involved going with other kids who had made a decision, talking with another Awana leader and praying to invite Jesus to come into your heart.

They also served cookies in this room to kids who made decisions to follow Jesus. Some weeks when I was hankering for dessert, I would make a decision to follow Jesus, go to the room, pray the sinner's prayer once again and eat a cookie. At some point the Awana leaders noticed that I had become a Christian on multiple occasions. They pulled me aside to let me know that I really only needed to pray once to invite Jesus into my heart. I was embarrassed and guilty and slightly relieved because even though I wanted a cookie, I wanted more to know that I actually did belong to Jesus. I wanted to make sure I was enough as a Christian and that God knew I *reaaaaaally* wanted him in my life. My faith as a child didn't seem like enough compared to Alison, who could memorize and recite all the Bible verses each week, or to Nicole, who never seemed to get in trouble or talk too much like I did. How could I be sure that I really was enough for Jesus? That I really was "in"? Like Martin Luther struggling in the tower of Wittenberg to believe that God's grace was enough to save him, I was having my own eight-year-old existential faith crisis to believe that I didn't have to do anything to earn God's love or grace for me.

All In

That summer my mom took my brother and sister and me to the UP County Fair—a big deal in the Upper Peninsula of Michigan, which didn't have a lot of entertainment in the 1980s. As we walked down the dusty paths past the Tilt-A-Whirl and cotton-candy trailers, begging my mom for sugary drinks sold in brightly colored animal-shaped bottles, she saw a trailer marked "Gospel Trailer" run by Child Evangelism Fellowship. My parents, especially my mom, was always one for Jesus experiments—going to a Presbyterian church and participating in Bible studies, but also joining Women's Aglow, a charismatic women's ministry focused on speaking in tongues. As kids we got to join them in all of these experiments, seeing a broad view of what the church was. Munching snow cones, we went into the gospel trailer and sat down in the stuffy room to hear the presentation of the gospel. After showing us the flannel cutouts of how Jesus came to earth, died on the cross to take away our sin and makes a place for us to be with God in heaven, the woman asked, "Do you want to invite Jesus into your heart, Jessica?"

"Oh, I've already done that," I replied. "I do that every week at Awana, actually." This was probably news to my mom, who thought Awana had sparked more of an interest in ventriloquism for me than in Jesus.

What the woman did next was something that has stuck with me for my entire life. "Jessica, get up. Go outside the room, just outside the door." I stood just outside the door in the small, warm trailer. "Come in," she said. I took a step forward across the threshold of the door. "Come in," she said again. I took another step forward. "Come in." Confused why she kept telling me to come in, I took a really big step forward just to make sure she knew I could hear her and follow instructions. My siblings stared at me, nibbling their snow cones. "Come in." She motioned with her hand to come farther into the room. I took another step forward, so close that I was now right next to the lady.

"Okay, I'm as far as I can come in," I said, wondering why she had me take so many steps.

"Jessica," she asked, "when did you enter the room?"

I thought for a minute. "I was in the room when I entered the door," I responded.

"Yes," she said. "When we invite Jesus into our hearts to be our Savior and Lord, we don't have to keep inviting him. He is with you. He'll never leave you. There is nothing you can do to change that. He came into your life when you said yes to him. You don't need to prove that you really want him by continuing to invite him into your heart."

That day in the stuffy trailer I felt assurance for the first time that Jesus loved me. I didn't need to do anything to get his attention or prove to him that I really wanted him in my life. I had said yes to his invitation to be my Savior and Lord and that was enough. It was enough that I had taken one step forward of obedience to say yes. That small step was the beginning for me to understand what it meant to live out the gospel. It didn't matter how much I did for Jesus to prove to him that I loved him or was good enough for him. Romans 1:16-17 says, "For I am not ashamed of the gospel, because it is the power of God that brings salvation to everyone who believes: first to the Jew, then to the Gentile. For in the gospel the righteousness of God is revealed—a righteousness that is by faith from first to last, just as it is written: 'The righteous will live by faith.'" The small faith I had as a child was enough for Jesus. He was asking me just to believe.

For all I know, the lady from Child Evangelism Fellowship felt discouraged that more people chose to ride the Ferris wheel than come into the gospel trailer, and annoyed that she had to sit inside on a sunny day. Perhaps she thought that her small step of obedience to share the gospel at a county fair didn't make any difference. It didn't really matter what she thought, because her willingness to be obedient and share the gospel made a difference in my life forever. It's likely that she never knew that her obedience that day sparked a love in a young girl to tell many, many others about the love of Jesus.

We have a choice every day to seek him and ask him, *How do I best live out and share your gospel story today?* That is what evangelism is about—unleashing the gospel story in our own lives in such a way that we flourish and the people around us are drawn in because they see the tiptoes, the strides and leaps of faith when we step out with beautiful feet to share good news. We are meant to respond to others in and through the love of Christ, not because we want to do something flashy, sacrificial or dutiful to God. As a community we need to celebrate the small and the big stories of faithfulness because it's not just the dramatic sacrifices that Jesus wants us to make—it's also the small steps of obedience to follow him.

Author Robert Louis Stevenson is credited to have said, "Don't judge each day by the harvest you reap but by the seeds that you plant." It seems in the church these days we forget that nothing grows unless you plant seeds. The harvest seems to be the only thing that's celebrated rather than the small steps of obedience by a whole community. When we only celebrate the harvest rather than the seeds we plant, we give the impression that only what becomes "successful" is what matters in life and evangelism.

Am I Enough?

There is a frantic energy in the church that makes us feel like we have to measure up and become some sort of super apostle. Like fearful pigeons we flock to the most immediate need, saying yes to others so we don't disappoint or seem uncaring. Even if it is something we don't enjoy, aren't good at or know someone else would be better suited for, saying yes seems like the Christian thing to do. I mean, c'mon—it's for *Jesus*.

For those of us who struggle with perfectionism, fear or feelings of inadequacy, this is especially dangerous. And I'd say just about every woman I know struggles with those things. If we can't measure up to the people whose books we read or whose sermons we hear at conferences, or the women who seem to have boundless time and energy to volunteer for afterschool programs, neighborhood potlucks or doing pro bono work at law clinics, what's the point in even trying? We end up burning ourselves out trying to be like them and do what they do, or we give up and are hopeless, believing nothing we do will make any difference. We waste a lot of mental energy and indulge in a lot of self-hatred when we compare ourselves to what other Christian women are doing. And when we're caught up in the comparisons and fear, we miss out on what God is inviting us to do and how he wants to love us and send us to love others. We need to stop and ask, *Jesus, how do you want* me *to use my beautiful feet to speak about and demonstrate your love to others?*

A few years ago a family in our church asked for prayer for their adoption process for a little girl with special needs from China.[2] I immediately felt resentment rise inside me when I saw the wife and husband crying, all the people in our congregation praying for them and hugging them after their tearful testimony about God's call to love orphans, and the slideshow of the bake sale their daughter's Sunday school class was holding to raise money for the adoption costs. It was so dramatic, so sacrificial, such a public display of what Christian love looks like. People looked at their family and embraced them, saying things like, "You guys are living out such a radical faith. It's amazing to see how you're trusting Jesus to do such a big thing for him."

Seeing all of this made me sick with envy. I wanted to be that kind of Christian: the sacrificial, blended, orphan-loving, kingdom-of-God kind of family. I wanted my family to be the kind that people look at and think, "Wow, they *really* love Jesus.

They adopt *orphans*. How cool are they?" With amazement people would ask me how I learned to braid the hair of my biracial daughter or how I helped my adopted son to learn about his cultural heritage as an Eastern European. I just would shrug it off, smile and say something casual like, "That's what Christians do. We love orphans and widows."

Looking at that family in church, I realized it wasn't that I wanted to adopt orphans. That's not what Jesus was calling our family to do. The thing I wanted was the kind of love that was showy—to have some sort of lavish demonstration of faith that would make people really take notice and question their own willingness to make loving sacrifices. My own sacrifices felt small in comparison, and I wondered if I was living out a radical enough faith. Having a neighbor over for pizza seemed like such a small thing compared with the financial, emotional and spiritual costs that this family was making to live out their faith. I felt unimportant, unspiritual and jealous, and I questioned if my faith and efforts were enough for Jesus.

This is the kind of disgustingness that happens when we get trapped in Christian comparisons and focus on how other people are following Jesus rather than what it means for us to follow him. We obsess about what we *want* our lives to look like instead of how God is inviting us to follow him right now. We focus on how big and showy our demonstration of love is rather than being grateful that Jesus loves us and chooses to use us to love others. We begin to believe the lie that we aren't enough and that nothing we do to share Jesus is enough.

You Must Follow Me

Jesus sends us to love others in ordinary and strange places, like a trailer at a county fair or adoption of special-needs kids from China. We must pay attention to the things that light us up with love or

churn resentment or anger within us. These are clue[s]
wants us to follow him if we take the time to reflect [on]
that way. For me, the moment of envy while watching ... orphan
saga was a realization of something inside of me that was dis-
content about how I was living out my faith. I felt like I could do
more and wanted to be used to care for marginalized children. The
desire was to live with more of a sacrificial faith, but I needed to
reflect more on how God was inviting me to follow him in that
desire rather than being resentful and envious of how he was
working that out in the lives of others.

When we have these moments of resentment or desire we can
begin to recognize how God wants to use us to reach his world.
Often we leave it at the resentment and end up filling our schedules
with a bunch of stuff to make us feel important and sacrificial
rather than stopping to ask, *Jesus, why am I so upset about this? What
are you trying to tell me with these feelings of envy, joy, indifference or
excitement?* In those moments we can ask him to give us clarity on
what it means to follow him in everyday life in how he is calling us
to love others. I love how Jesus responds to Peter in John 21 when
Peter is caught up in worrying about the faith of the other disciples,
especially John. Jesus says, "What is that to you? You must follow
me" (John 21:22). Jesus hits it dead center when Peter begins to
question the call on John's life. He essentially answers him, "Hey
man, what are you doing to follow me? Chill out. Don't worry
about him. You must follow me."

You must follow me. Not, "You must do what other people are
doing" or, "Following me looks like the thing you most hate to do
(or love to do)." Following Jesus means listening and obeying him
when he invites us to love. We learn how to follow him by spending
time in Scripture and community, exploring what life with him
looks like by opening our eyes to our neighborhoods, campuses and
cities to ask, *Jesus, how are you inviting me to love people here?* We

follow him by exploring our skills, interests and passions, and the needs of the people and world around us. These small acts of love we demonstrate every day should be like an irresistible beat that lingers after our interactions with people, leaving them wondering what that catchy song was and how they can hear it again.

Jesus may never call my husband and me to adopt orphans. But he invites us every day to love the neighbor kids who come over to play with our son, to stop and have a conversation with the other parents from my son's preschool instead of rushing home, and to pray for and financially support Ikuzwe, the Compassion child from Rwanda my son picked to sponsor. It may not be flashy. We will likely never have a touching video about our sacrifices to love others shown on a Sunday morning at church, but that's not the point, is it? Jesus' instruction—"You must follow me"—is the point.

You must follow Jesus. There is no one else who can do that for you. You must listen to him. You must find out how he has wired you, the passions he's given you, how your heart breaks for the world. What makes your heart leap with joy when you get to lead, participate in or implement whatever it is you've been dreaming about? When we ignore or minimize our desires in following Jesus or compare what it looks like for others to follow him, it leads us to despair, anger and frustration. If we don't take the time to discover and recognize these things we begin to resent others because of how they are following Jesus. But hopefully it drives us to figure out how to use our own beautiful feet.

Love Hurts

My friends Jacki and Patrick chose to open their home to foster babies. Yes, babies. Babies who cry all night and wake up every three hours because they're hungry or need a diaper change. Babies who are so newly born that they aren't even that cute yet and still look like squishy potatoes. It takes great love to open your heart up to enter into a legal agreement knowing that the love you pour out may only be for a short time and there may well be the pain of giving up the baby you have cared for since they were tiny. So each week in small group we prayed with Patrick and Jacki that they would be able to keep Mya, their foster daughter.

God in his goodness allowed Mya to become their daughter. And during that time, Jacki unexpectedly got pregnant. Our friends at MOPS would tease her about how crazy her life was going to be with a one-and-a-half-year-old and a newborn. Mya was adopted, then their son, Eli, was born, and then five weeks later, they got a call. Mya's birth mom had just had another baby; somehow Patrick's and Jacki's names were still in the foster-care system as caregivers. Would they be willing to foster and possibly adopt Mya's newborn sister? A week later Jacki and Patrick had three kids under eighteen months old. No one at MOPS teased Jacki anymore about how crazy her life was going to be—we were simply amazed and somewhat horrified that she said yes to having two newborns and a one-and-a-half-year-old.

The love Patrick and Jacki have poured out isn't a showy kind of love. It's a day-in, day-out choice to say, "Jesus, I trust you though I am exhausted, though I am resentful at the birth mom for making poor choices, though I fantasize about being able to have an uninterrupted night of sleep. Though I'm barely hanging on and wonder if I'll be able to get through today. Though our marriage is difficult right now because of the stress of caring for three screaming kids every day and night." It has been sobering to watch Jacki and Patrick invite their community to pour out love on their kids because they know they can't do it alone. It hasn't been easy for them but they have still said yes to following Jesus into the daily grind and glory of love. It's also been amazing to hear their stories about how people far from God are stunned to hear about the ways they are trusting Jesus with loving their three kids and the way their community is providing for them.

This kind of love shocks people because it is outside our own capabilities to love—it speaks to our need for a God who connects us to himself as the source of love. I wasn't jealous of Jacki and Patrick, unlike the other family, because the love they expressed was so ordinary. It wasn't about any flashy show of following Jesus. It was simply about saying yes; saying yes to Jesus and his love in every 2:00 a.m. feeding, in every fit of crying tantrums, in every load of baby clothes soaked in urine. Saying yes to the love of Jesus in the daily sacrifice of dying to self. No one is jealous of this kind of love because it is painful, requires sacrifice and is unseen by most people.

This kind of love is staggering. It doesn't pack up when the fundraiser is done, when people get excited about the next cause and forget about the one they were supporting last week. Most of the time following Jesus is about putting one foot in front of the other and saying, *Yes, yes, yes, Lord. I will follow you. No matter where you lead, no matter what it looks like. I don't need to worry about what the path of others is like, I can focus on you, your love and your leading.* It hurts to say yes when love isn't reciprocated, but that's the kind of crazy love Jesus has for us and for the world. The love of Jesus tells us, "I love you, no matter what. No matter how angry you are, how filled with resentment, pain, shame, fear and bitterness. I love you. Don't hide from me. I am enough for you. I have enough love for you. I have enough love for you to give to others."

Mother Teresa is attributed to saying, "We can do no great things, only small things with great love." We can do no great things. In fact, Jesus says in John 15:5 that "apart from me you can do nothing." Jesus doesn't tack on any words to *nothing*: he doesn't say you can do "nothing significant," "nothing great" or "nothing influential." He just says, "apart from me you can do nothing." Straight-up nothing. Nada. Zero. Zilch.

We need to be connected to the source of love. Because the point isn't to do great things; the point is to love greatly. It's scary to love because love isn't a project. It doesn't hide behind professionalism or structures. Love permeates people's lives to the point where they respond with joy and gratitude because their hearts are brimming with the kind of love only Jesus can provide. Jesus fills us and moves us out into his world to speak and demonstrate this love to others. That's far more amazing than anything anyone can ever accomplish. Through us, God is mobilizing his kingdom coming here on earth as it is in heaven.

Experiments in Love

In their book *On the Verge*, Alan Hirsch and Dave Ferguson use the word *simplex* to describe what it means to follow Jesus with the statement "Jesus is Lord."[3] These three words are simple. Jesus is the leader of our lives and world. Yet the implications for this statement are profound and far-reaching. Jesus' command in Mark 12:30-31 says, "'Love the Lord your God with all your heart and with all your soul and with all your mind and with all your strength.' The second is this: 'Love your neighbor as yourself.' There is no commandment greater than these." Easy peasy, right?

Jesus' instructions are general: love. Confess and believe he is Lord. He knows the best ways to love people, for us to utilize all that we have and all that we are to love others. With his direction as the leader of our lives and in our communities, we get to work out the specifics of what that looks like, what our capabilities and passions are, and what needs around us can be met. Since we are creatures of habit we typically do what is most comfortable and familiar to us. Yet discovering how Jesus is inviting you to follow him should look like an experiment in love.

Following Jesus will involve pain and sacrifice. But more often than not I've found that my heart blossoms with love when I consider how to best love others and act upon it. When I spend time with Jesus, remembering his shocking love for me, my feet are quick to respond because I realize that he can help me to love and I don't have to do it by myself or with my own strength. This is the paradox of faith—that spending time with Jesus helps us to turn in love to serve others.

On Valentine's Day a few years ago I was feeling resentful that my husband was working out of town, that he would likely be too tired to pick up any sort of gift or be emotionally present to me. I had been home alone on a snowy weekend with our two-year-old son, Reuben, and every Zales and Kay Jewelers commercial that came on made me sink even further into self-pity. *Every kiss begins with Kay? More like every Kick-me-when-I'm-down begins with K.*

Even though I lay on the couch dreaming of the showy, sparkly ring I wouldn't receive, the Holy Spirit convicted me and invited me to consider worshiping God and serving others rather than feeling sorry for myself or being bummed about the gifts I wasn't going to get. He reminded me that I had a son I could love and consider how to best serve, and a husband who was going to come home tired. Was he going to come home to a resentful, snippy wife or a place of love and rest?

That day I chose to take Reuben to the zoo in Grand Rapids to see the penguins. At the time he was obsessed with penguins and would shriek with laughter and excitement every time he saw a toy penguin or one in a cartoon. Tromping down the snowy path, with his little mittened hand in mine, we made our way to the penguin house. Together, we watched the penguins dive and waddle, listening to their echoing honks and seeing them gulp down tiny silver fish that the zookeeper threw to them. We were both delighted to see the raucous enjoyment of the penguins on such a dull, gray February day. Afterward we went to the craft store and picked up some simple half-price Valentine's Day decorations to welcome Daddy home and made some cupcakes.

A day that could have been spent stewing in resentment became a day of gratitude to love my son and husband by serving them. I could have come up with a list of the reasons why I should have been served rather than serve others. But because Jesus is Lord, his love can overcome resentment, fear and indifference in my life. Because he is Lord, a holiday devoted to "love" that makes most people feel sad and inadequate actually turned into a choice to love my family.

Saying yes that day looked like moving from self-pity to sacrificial love, focusing on how I could care for someone else rather than what I wasn't getting. I used my beautiful feet to go and see penguins with my son and bake cupcakes for our family. It wasn't big or dramatic. No one could see what was happening inside of me except God. But I was aware of the change in my heart, and it made my day a lot more enjoyable. I turned from self-pity toward self-sacrifice (though can you really consider baking and eating cupcakes a sacrifice?). I was able to create a memory with my son and husband that I'm thankful for rather than stewing in resentment about not getting what I wanted. Incidentally, that day Dave did bring me home a pot of yellow tulips. And instead of feeling entitled to them, I was able to receive them as a gift with gratitude.

"This is not the adolescent love of eros, the desire to acquire, the egocentric appetite. This is the love of the other for its own sake, the care for someone else's feelings and preferences and needs. This is the forgetting of self and the enjoyment of service."[4] This is how theologian John Stackhouse describes Jesus' command to love God and neighbor as self. He goes on to ask how our churches would be transformed if we asked the question of how to best worship God and serve others rather than do what we prefer.

Just because you like doing something or it's the way things have always been done in your church doesn't mean that it is God's best way to love others through you. And just because something makes you uncomfortable or scared doesn't mean that God isn't using it for his good purposes in your life or church. This is not an easy five-step plan; it's not a set of crafted studies that will be the silver bullet you might be looking for to invigorate your faith and witness or congregation. It's love and faith, submission and sacrifice, boldness and humility, all wrapped up together in asking Jesus, *How can I best speak about and demonstrate your love to others today?*

Just Experiment

Some of us love to study Scripture and could reach out to others by offering to do an investigative Bible study with them, passing along an inspiring sermon or giving a friend a devotional to explore Jesus. Others of us like structures and tradition because they help us connect with a faith that has persevered for centuries. We can take part in this by praying a liturgy, enjoying beautiful stained glass windows in a cathedral that help us reflect on the glory of God, or singing hymns that have been written by steadfast saints from long ago. Nadia Bolz-Weber, in her raw and hilarious book *Pastrix*,[5] describes discovering the tradition of liturgy as letting the ancestors of the faith have a say in shaping her views and practices of following Jesus. In a chaotic, unpredictable world where everything is marketed to make things easier, cooler and more appealing, participating in an ancient tradition of praying the divine hours or using the Book of Common Prayer can feel like a balm of authenticity and solidarity with other Christians who have worshiped using these practices for generations.

As someone who loves liturgy as much as I love gospel choirs, my understanding of how to connect with others about Jesus has grown because of trying new ways to connect with him. Worship isn't just for our own benefit to experience the diverse and beautiful ways God has made this world, but also it's a way for us to realize that there are myriad ways to help people hear about and experience the love of Jesus. When we connect with Jesus he helps us become comfortably uncomfortable in taking risks to love others and we grow in our obedience to follow him.

Try things out to see what fits with who God has made you to be, what you're passionate about and what you have the capabilities to do. If you're trying something outside your faith background, whether you're a Christian or not, that's worth some self-reflection. Ask yourself, "What about this makes me feel uncomfortable? How can I be open to Jesus to connect in a new way? How might this experience help me to love someone else?"

While you might not connect with Jesus through liturgy, gospel music, silence or singing in another language, many other people do. We aren't meant to share the message of a particular church tradition or denomination; we are meant to share the gospel message. We become imperialistic and judgmental when we believe there are only certain ways to experience Jesus or worship him. I often encourage the college students I work with to experiment in their spirituality by trying new things as Christians, whether that's service, prayer, evangelism or worship. One student at a Christian college where I preached took issue with the word *experiment*. I reminded him that I wasn't inviting him to experiment with LSD or heroin; I was inviting him to experiment with Jesus.

For people who aren't yet Christians it can be a powerful thing to begin to experiment with spiritual practices that help them not simply learn about Jesus, but experience what it means to follow him. At a conference I led for students who were exploring Jesus, we spent time packing shoeboxes full of toys, toothbrushes and crayons for Operation Christmas Child. When I asked the students how they felt during the experience, one student piped up and said, "You know, I really like to gamble. Seeing the video of how happy the kids were receiving the shoeboxes made me think about how I could use that money to care for people who don't

have much instead of using forty dollars to gamble every month."
Instead of just learning that Jesus wants us to care for the poor,
he had an experience of what it felt like to care for the poor because Jesus loves them. That weekend, that same student chose to
follow Jesus. We invited him into an experiment of love, and Jesus
challenged him to love like he does. Regardless of where you are
spiritually, we need to experiment as individuals and churches
because God has limitless ways to connect with us and for us to
love others. He longs for more for the people in our lives than
good deeds, awkwardly shared gospel scripts or weird apologetic
arguments that try to convince someone that Jesus is more than
a fairytale.

We don't lack for methods or strategies for sharing our faith. I
think the bigger problem is that our capacity to love is far too small
for the mission into which God has
invited us. Evangelism freaks us out

> Our capacity to love is
> far too small for the mission
> into which God has invited us.

because we are afraid. We are afraid
of being judged, afraid of saying the
wrong thing, afraid of offending
others. Serving others can be uncomfortable, cause conflict and
bring out our insecurities. Scripture tells us that perfect love casts
out fear. Our love is far from perfect. We mess up bigtime every
day. So how do we get more love? We go back to the source of love.
Jesus is the one who connects us to the God who, as Sally Lloyd-
Jones writes in *The Jesus Storybook Bible*, loves us with a "Never
Stopping, Never Giving Up, Unbreaking, Always and Forever
Love."[6] When we rely on ourselves, we get caught up in wanting
to do something big, something great for God, rather than being
caught up in love with him. Or we underestimate the small things
we do to love others on a daily basis. God uses ordinary people and
ordinary things. Not great, spectacular people who are articulate,
impressive and well connected. He uses fishermen and wandering

Israelites, college students and refugees, little children and fast-food employees.

We don't need to do anything big and impressive to love other people. We don't need to do anything to impress God. All he asks is that we confess and believe that Jesus is Lord and then orient our lives around this profound declaration. Most of us just need to love greatly in the small things God has given each of us. Perfect love casts out fear. Love casts out fear when we take a risk and offer to pray for a neighbor who is frustrated with her job. Love casts out fear when we invite a classmate to church and then to share a meal together afterward. Love casts out fear when we sit in silence with someone who is grieving, knowing that the best love we can offer is simply to be there. Whether it's standing up in front of a classroom to share about your faith in Jesus or choosing to use your vacation time to volunteer as a construction worker in Haiti, the love of God is able to silence our fears and give us more love. No one is too important to love. No one is too insignificant to love.

Interpret Your Actions

"Faith without works is dead." People often quote James 2 as a cop-out to avoid sharing their faith verbally. The hope is that, without our sharing the gospel outright, our friends will somehow catch on that we love Jesus and that his love compels us to serve others. More often than not, however, people interpret that you're just really nice and a good person. But Romans 3:12 says, "There is no one who does good, not even one."

We are able to love because God first loved us. Whether you're bringing soup to a sick friend, volunteering to clean up a local park or helping at-risk kids learn how to read, it's a great starting place to talk about how God created us to love and serve others. When someone expresses gratitude for your service, say something simple like, "I'm grateful for the ways God has cared for me and I want to show that love to others" or, "That's what people who follow Jesus do: love and serve others" or, "I've got some massive love for Jesus and am just passing along his goodness to others in the form of chili and cornbread." This helps people to connect service to love of Jesus, demonstrates an active faith and can raise curiosity about how the love of Jesus compels us to serve.

Response

We need Jesus to change us from the inside out so that we love people well in word and deed. Take a few moments and choose one of the response activities below. Reflecting is part of how we recognize the presence of God in our lives. Even if you need to come back to it later, take ten to twenty minutes thinking and praying about the love of God in your own life. Try something new to experience the presence of Jesus. You will find that God is much bigger than you imagined him to be and that his love stretches to you and others in profound and creative ways.

Explore other Jesus experiments. Read Luke 21:1-4, John 6:1-15 or Acts 6:1-7. What do you notice about Jesus' response or the communities' response to the people in these passages? You may not feel like you have enough to give others—not enough time, resources or love. Yet Jesus calls all of us to give of what we have. Confess the places you feel like you aren't enough, where you have been afraid to love others, hesitant to become involved in peoples' lives and offer what you do have. Spend time thanking Jesus that he loves you just as you are and can use you just as you are and with what you have to love and serve other people.

Pick something small. Call a friend with whom you haven't talked in a while to see how they're doing and pray for them. Spend some time playing with your kids or being with your friends and be present to them rather than checking your phone. Pick up bagels for your colleagues at work and be grateful that God has given you the resources to do so—and be content with that rather than wanting people to express gratitude to you. Tell someone who is far from God about how Jesus is giving you more love for yourself and other people.

Try something new to experience the presence of Jesus. Ask someone from a different Christian tradition from yours to teach you about how they experience Jesus. Visit a Greek Orthodox Church, sing worship songs in Spanish or Korean, sit in silence. Serve homeless kids in your city. Pray with your hands in the air, aloud with a group of others, or face-down on the ground. Fast from food or the Internet. Margot Starbuck's *Small Things with Great Love* or Richard Foster's *Celebration of Discipline* are great resources for trying some new Jesus experiments.

Are You a Peacock or a Pigeon?

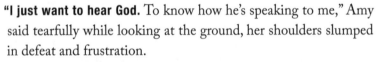

"I just want to hear God. To know how he's speaking to me," Amy said tearfully while looking at the ground, her shoulders slumped in defeat and frustration.

We were at the Urbana Student Missions Conference in St. Louis. Amy, who had come from the Bible Belt area of the North (otherwise known as West Michigan), had just recommitted her life to Jesus. She had gone to church her whole life, had all the right answers and knew that God theoretically was present, yet she still felt like she was missing something. Her life felt empty in the midst of a missions convention where God seemed to be speaking to everyone but her.

I could relate to Amy too. And so could many of my friends who felt distant from God even though they were having quiet times, going to church or serving others in their city. Whether we voiced them or not, we had questions: *Do any of the Christian things I'm doing make any difference? Why do I struggle to hear God's voice? How am I supposed to tell people about Jesus when I feel so far away from him? If I slow down to be with God will it make any difference in my life or the lives of others?*

I thought about my friend Laurie, whose mother, Jan, happily attended a Christian church for thirty years and got up early to study the Bible every morning. After Laurie's decade of largely ineffective attempts at the same, those patterns did not provide Laurie the peace and fulfillment that they did her mother. She felt like she was just going along with what she had been taught instead of finding a way to genuinely be in God's presence. Laurie was struggling with whether or not she believed all of what she was hearing in church—and yet relationally she felt internal pressure to withhold her doubts about Jesus as the only way to God. She had so many friends with a wide range of beliefs, and friends who devoutly practiced other religions. On a playdate in the Rockefeller Greenhouses with our kids on a cold winter day we walked among the steamy rooms filled with verdant plants and spicy flowers.[1] Laurie shared that it was hard to see herself following Jesus in the ways she had seen it presented—everything seemed too conservative, too rigid, not connected enough to what was actually happening in the world, in her family or even in her own body and spirit.

"I'm just not sure if I buy all this stuff," she confessed to me as we pulled our kids back from trying to plunge into the koi pond.

"Well, why don't you just stop? What's keeping you going to church or reading the Bible if you feel like it doesn't make any difference?" I asked.

She shrugged, and with a pained look on her face said, "It feels too costly to walk away from it all. It's comfortable; it's how I was raised. I'll make people angry and disappointed if I decide to stop the whole Christian thing. No matter what I decide I'm disappointing someone—friends might think I'm intolerant of their beliefs if I say that Jesus is the only way to God. My family would be disappointed because they'd think I threw away all the spiritual investment they put into my life as a child. I literally think it would kill my grandfather." I could see the tension flicker across her face.

"Is it going to be more costly," I asked, "to pretend like you don't have questions, doubts and fears, to ignore them and go through the motions?" Though we were right in the middle of a serious conversation, my son Ozzy spotted a butterfly and was excitedly trying to get our attention to watch it drift through the steamy haze of the greenhouse. Though we didn't get to finish our conversation that day, Laurie and I continued to ask the question, "Why does our fear hold us back from pursuing Jesus?" Even in our brief conversation we talked about how it was scary to disappoint other people if our faith didn't look similar to theirs, how it was uncomfortable to voice our doubts, questions, insecurities and fears to God and to each other. Though Laurie longed for something different in her spiritual life, she felt immobilized by fear of what others would think or say about her, feeling alone in her doubts and the discomfort of exploring something outside of the options she had experienced in various churches.

Going Through the Motions

Jesus is able to connect with us in a personal way because he knows us and loves us. Yet many times we believe that following him has to look a certain way. Our fear holds us back both from taking risks to spend time with Jesus and from following him into the adventure of loving people. It's scary to step out to speak about Jesus, to live a life that is obedient to him when it means looking and living really differently. It's easier just to go through the motions rather than pause to ask, *Jesus, how are you calling me to follow you? What do you want to speak into my life right now? How are you calling me to love and serve others in a practical way?* It's also scary to honestly bring our doubts, fears and hesitations to him in part because that's not what "a good Christian woman" does. It takes time to reflect on where we are at with Jesus, who he is making us to become and the steps of obedience he is inviting us into. Living out and sharing our faith is birthed from a loving relationship with God in which we are able to bring all that we are—hopes, fears, longings and doubts—to our friend Jesus and explore those things together.

Colors on the Page

My friend Naomi once offered me her home as a quiet space for prayer and reflection. I was worried about taking a few hours away that morning to pray and journal. Instead I was thinking about the emails that needed to be sent, the students I was going to meet with later that day and the week's worth of dishes that had piled up in my kitchen. (You know it's bad when you've been eating cereal for dinner because you don't have any clean dishes in which to cook.) I knew none of those things would change if I took a few hours to pray, and I hoped to overcome the crushing tiredness I was feeling. My life felt out of balance, my schedule too frantic and my body weary. Even the things that were important to me—having friends over for dinner, going hiking or having a clean bathroom to enjoy while I soaked in the tub—took a back burner to the all-consuming work of ministry on a college campus. I was putting in the time doing the "right things" but I felt empty, angry and like Jesus was far away.

At Naomi's house I settled onto the red wing-backed chair in her quiet, bookshelf-lined den. I glanced through the poetry and photography books my friend had laid out to inspire me. They looked more inviting than the devotional and Bible tucked into my black messenger bag. I thought, *You're such a loser. You can't even bring yourself to have a quiet time and crack open your Bible. What kind of a minister are you?* Pangs of guilt shot through me for feeling not only like a loser but also like a hypocrite since my job was to help students connect with Jesus and tell others about how amazing he is. A box of colored pencils, markers and paper lay next to the books. Without thinking much about it, I picked up a few markers and a blank sheet of paper and began to draw. The silence in the room was unnerving. I wasn't used to it, and I felt like I needed to do something to push the negative thoughts out of my mind and focus on good Jesusy thoughts instead.

I didn't have any image in mind as I chose a green marker and began drawing lines across the page. Slowly, the emerald lines curved as I continued to sketch, tracing the lines over and over again, the repetitive movement almost feeling like a liturgy, like my joining in with something that many had done before. The shape began to look like a bird; the emerald green reminded me of a peacock. I added some blue plumes, a long ornate tail with turquoise and red lines. The colors popped out in contrast with one another. I drew and drew, the colors deepening, the peacock becoming clearer. It didn't occur to me until later that I wasn't berating myself for not doing a "real Christian" thing. Nor was I wasting time worrying that it might look more like a chicken than a peacock to other people who saw my sketch. I was lost in the delight of creating and enjoying the presence of God while doing so.

As I laid the marker down and looked at what had emerged on the page, I sensed God speaking to me through the picture. He knew me. He loved me. There was no guilt in how I was spending time with him. He invited me to be with him and enjoy our time together.[2]

I had unsuccessfully tried to be one of those Christians who gets up at 6 a.m. to study a chapter of the Bible every day, to diligently pray for ten people in my life to become Christians and to like Christian music (usually Pink, Stevie Wonder or David Bowie won out). But recently images had begun to appear as I prayed, images that led me into worship of God and a connectedness with him that felt fresh and vibrant. I was having genuine encounters with God like I'd never had before. I wasn't just reading Scripture; the

Holy Spirit was drawing me into the text to see the dust on the disciples' feet, to feel the tension in the room when the woman came to wash Jesus' feet, and to linger on words and phrases that I had never noticed before.

I had been encouraged to study the Bible inductively, to dig for meaning in the text, to use Bible commentaries, but I had never been taught to invite the Holy Spirit to use my imagination, my creativity and my senses to help me experience Jesus in prayer or Scripture. At the time I didn't know that St. Ignatius was one of the foremost people to engage creativity with prayer and Scripture reading. Gary Neal Hansen, in *Kneeling with Giants*, writes, "Ignatius's prayer of the senses allows the Word of God to be the forum for prayer as real conversation, asking God questions, knowing we are heard and actually hearing answers."[3]

I stared at the bright swirl of a bird and sensed God saying to me in a bold but loving way, "You are a peacock, not a pigeon. Stop trying to hide who you are. I meant for you to show the brilliance of how I've created you for my glory. Strut and all. You are not meant to blend in."

The Holy Spirit brought to mind Joseph in the book of Genesis and the dreams God had given him (see Genesis 37-45). He wore his flashy rainbow robe that made him stick out like a brilliant bird among his brothers and anyone else who saw him. He didn't blend in. Though it would have been easy to simply look at his external appearance and judge him as flashy, Joseph was a peacock because of how he demonstrated bold and extravagant faith in God. He was a peacock because that's who the Lord called him to be. He was a peacock when he was just a boy. But being a peacock wasn't a glamorous experience for Joseph. It hurt. It involved suffering through messed-up relationships, loneliness, fear and doubt. It involved anger and betrayal. Joseph's experience of following the Lord includes an astounding amount of highs and lows. It was painful to be sold into slavery by his brothers. To be wrongfully accused of raping Potiphar's wife and thrown in prison. To languish for years in that same prison hoping to be remembered by the cupbearer whose dream he interpreted. To deal with the pain, confusion and sadness of seeing his brothers begging him for food during the famine, then wrestle with whether or not to be merciful to them or to exact vengeance that perhaps he had been imagining for years.

For Joseph, being a peacock wasn't about the external things in his life or the relationships he had with others. He enjoyed his father's love and approval (Genesis 37:3); he was a dreamer (Genesis 37:5); he became a powerful attendant in Egypt after coming in as a foreign slave (Genesis 39:2-4); he was a stone-cold fox (Genesis 39:6); he had the most luxury clothing and jewelry (Genesis 41:42). But being a peacock didn't mean looking a certain way; it meant living a certain way. For Joseph and the many other peacocks in Scripture and in history, it meant living with the faith that the Lord was with him. Joseph believed and acted upon his belief in the Lord, trusting him whether in plenty or in want, whether betrayed by people or seeking approval with important people. Joseph could have acted out of fear and anger because of his circumstances, or brought those fears to the Lord and asked, *Are you here with me? Why is this happening to me?* One of the most often quoted lines from Joseph reveals his deep faith that the Lord was with him, for him and guiding him. That he was able to deal with his anger and questions, and that his heart was transformed in the process of trusting God whether he was in a prison or a palace. At the end of Genesis when Joseph's brothers are afraid that he will hold a grudge and pay them back for the evil they did against him, Joseph tells them, "Don't be afraid. Am I in the place of God? You intended to harm me, but God intended it for good to accomplish what is now being done, the saving of many lives. So then, don't be afraid" (Genesis 50:19-21).

Be a Peacock, Not a Pigeon

That morning at Naomi's, tears welled up in my eyes and all I could do was lie face-down on the carpet, making a puddle of tears and marveling at how well Jesus knew exactly how to love me. The story of Joseph was profound and spoke to me in a way that colored my imagination of what the experience of following the Lord had been like for Joseph. He knew the stories I needed from his Word to live into who he was calling me to be. I exhaled the prayer, *Daaaaaaaannng, Jesus.*

Even in my tiredness and my inability to engage in the things I thought would bring me closer to him—Bible study, guided prayer, the latest devotional—he spoke. He spoke through my fears and insecurities, and he guided me in a gentle way that would get at the heart issues with which I was wrestling. I was afraid to be a peacock. Afraid of what others thought of me, afraid to be myself, afraid I wasn't enough, afraid that I was going to mess things up in my ministry, my family, my marriage, my body. I was cowering in fear and the crushing tiredness was the perfect façade to keep me ignorant of it until I actually stopped and let Jesus speak into it.

Staring at the peacock on the page I realized that my fear was eclipsing my belief that God was with me. It was strangling out the woman God was calling me to be, because I knew it would be uncomfortable, I would stick out, I would piss people off, just like Joseph did when he excitedly shared with others about what God spoke to him, unaware of any negative ramifications.

"Don't be afraid"—God's words to me through Joseph, the original peacock. He spoke in his Technicolor-Jesus way of popping out unexpectedly as he often likes to do. It wasn't until many years later I realized the irony that he spoke to me through a peacock, the showy male of the species, rather than the peahen. Jesus, such a jokester.

When we take the time to be with Jesus, inviting the Holy Spirit to guide our time rather than bringing an agenda of what we think God should do, he meets us in profound ways. He invites each of us to be a peacock in unique, painful and magnificent ways.

That was the prayer I prayed for Amy that day at Urbana: that Jesus would begin to pop out at her in Technicolor magnificence. I prayed she would begin to see the people he wanted her to connect with, serve and love, and to experience him in a way that spoke to who he made her to be. I don't know how Jesus worked this out in Amy's life, but I began to realize that there was something more to spending time with Jesus than getting through a bunch of spiritual disciplines and going through the motions of what a Christian life looks like. It wasn't about ignoring or suppressing my fears—it was about bringing them to Jesus and inviting him to guide me in the midst of them. I wanted a Technicolor faith like Joseph's, and it started to dawn on me that it would be out of my control if I was actually going to follow Jesus. It was going to be scary, uncomfortable, painful, magnificent, filled with joy and secure in the truth.

When it comes to evangelism, it is effortless to be a pigeon—to blend in, to not stand out because of your faith, to go through the motions and hope someone will notice that you love Jesus and then magically become a Christian because they saw you mowing your neighbor's lawn. Jesus' words to me—"You are a peacock, not a pigeon"—reminded me how tempting it is to be a pigeon and how we fall prey to it all the time, fearing that God is unable to use us because of our inadequacies or circumstances.

Once on a retreat I was frantically looking for the color red as I walked through the woods, because a friend had told me that God had used the color red to speak into significant areas in her life. At one point Jesus seemed to say, "Why are you looking for what I gave her? That isn't how I want to speak to you. Put down your expectations of what you want me to do and just spend time with me." I realized that I was afraid Jesus wouldn't speak to me so I tried to conjure my own profound experience. I think a lot of us do that because we're afraid that if we stop and wait to hear from God, or step out in faith to share him, he just won't show up.

What does it mean to be a pigeon? It means letting fear control you instead of letting Jesus lead you. It means putting more stock in our fears and inadequacies than the fact that God has exhorted us through his promise, "Be strong and courageous. Do not be afraid or terrified because of them, for the LORD your God goes with you; *he will never leave you nor forsake you*" (Deuteronomy 31:6). It means getting wrapped up in comparing ourselves to where other people are spiritually and telling ourselves, "I could never do that."

Joseph's words speak directly into our pigeon mentality: "Don't be afraid. Am I in the place of God? You intended to harm me, but God intended it for good to accomplish what is now being done, the saving of many lives. So then, don't be afraid" (Genesis 50:19-21). The mission and purpose of Jesus is to save many lives, both spiritually and physically. He longs to care for the drugged-out addict living on the street, the lonely businessman who fills his life with a packed schedule to feel needed, the child sex slave in Bolivia praying to be set free, the family that seems to be perfect but is imploding because of anger and abuse. And beautifully, remarkably he chooses to save lives as we speak about and demonstrate his love to others. He doesn't give a one-size-fits-all formula for how to become a peacock; he invites us to discover what it means as we spend time with him and take risks to step out and love others. Living out and sharing our faith is birthed from a loving relationship with God. Just like with Joseph, God has a unique story for you to tell and live out that demonstrates that God loves us. That's scary. That's unpredictable. That's incredible. That's vibrant.

> Living out and sharing our faith is birthed from a loving relationship with God.

Kill the Pigeon, Not the Peacock

When it comes to sharing our faith with others, we have many moments where we choose to be a pigeon rather than a peacock. They are the moments where we rationalize and talk ourselves out of the risk that Jesus is inviting us to take because it makes us feel scared or uncomfortable. Thoughts drift through our minds like, *My friends will think I'm weird if I try to talk to them about Jesus. It will be too awkward if I offer to pray for a friend who doesn't know Jesus. Nobody would want me to preach, so I won't offer. I can't be that kind of Christian woman, because following Jesus can look only this certain way,* as whatever stereotype of a Christian woman you have floats through your head. We choose to be content with living a bland life with a nominal faith, unremarkable in any way. And then we are sad or angry when we feel far from God, though he has been inviting us to follow him into a deeper relationship. When we refuse to follow Jesus into boldly and lovingly sharing him with others, we reject how he is inviting us to become a peacock. We reject the ways he uniquely wants to love us and meet us in the midst of fears, doubts and insecurities, demonstrating to us, "See! I *am* here! I'm *always* here!"

Instead of killing the peacock that God made us to be, we need to kill the pigeon impulse to blend in and live an unremarkable faith. Philosopher and theologian St. Catherine of Siena is said to have written, "Be who God meant you to be and you will set the world on fire!" Like St. Catherine of Siena and the fictional character Katniss Everdeen from *The Hunger Games*, setting the world on fire comes out of being, not doing. When we are who God meant us to be, we set the world ablaze wherever we go. It takes time to discover who God has made us to be and a will-

> Instead of killing the peacock that God made us to be, we need to kill the pigeon impulse to blend in and live an unremarkable faith.

ingness to try different ways to experience his presence. Becoming a peacock to boldly and lovingly speak about and demonstrate the love of Jesus requires time, pain and discomfort, yet it offers profound moments of love and joy.

Pressing Through a Pigeon Moment

As I closed my journal, I was amazed at how God had shown up that day at Naomi's. I was filled with gratitude. I was invigorated by how Jesus had met me in a creative way that helped me to tangibly experience his presence. As I left Naomi's house, I walked down the street looking forward to telling my husband about how my retreat had gone. I saw a rusty red Ford Escort pulled over with its hood up, the driver looking dejected.

Go lay hands on his car and pray for him, the Holy Spirit prompted me as I walked nearer.

No, that's weird, my pigeonlike thoughts began. *I'll just pray for him now. It's basically the same thing.* I walked past the car, smiling and nodding at the black man at the wheel, noticing he was eating beef jerky.

Go back and lay hands on his car and pray for him, the Holy Spirit nudged again.

My feathers were ruffled. I had just come from a time of silent prayer and I just wanted to relish the Jesusy goodness I had experienced that day.

Ugh. No, I thought. *It's my day off. And still, that's weird. What if nothing happens?*

I was about to turn the corner when I sensed the Holy Spirit saying to me again, *Go pray for him.* Sighing, I turned around, looked at the car and tried to figure out what I was going to say to this guy.

I walked up to the driver's side, where he was still eating his beef jerky, and asked him what was wrong with his car. I introduced myself and he told me his name was Richard. Wearing blue coveralls, he had been on his way to his second-shift job and, after getting gas, the car had conked out on him.

"Um, Richard," I said, "I know this might be weird, but I felt like God was telling me to come pray for you and your car. Would you be cool with that?"

Instantly he began to smile and said, "Yeah! I haven't been to church in a long time, but I'll take any help I can get!"

I laid my hand on the cold, discolored hood and prayed that the car would work and that Richard would be able to get to his job on time. I thanked God for Richard and prayed for him to have peace in a stressful situation. I prayed that God would provide for him exactly what he needed. And I really hoped that, when I said "amen," he would turn his key and the engine would roar to life. I began to imagine the awesome story I would tell my students about how prayer works and God blesses others through us when we take time to be with him.

Richard turned the key. Nothing happened. He thanked me and I said goodbye, smiling and waving as I headed home.

I felt disappointed and foolish as I walked home, but I also noticed that something inside me had changed in those hours with Jesus and the markers. Being with Jesus and experiencing his love for me in a tangible way had made me more aware of and obedient to the Holy Spirit's direction. It emboldened me to listen and obey his directions, even if they seemed weird and made me feel uncomfortable. If God had put this situation in my life just a few hours earlier, I would have been consumed with my mental to-do list and worried that I was running late to my friend's house (though can you really ever be late for a personal silent prayer time?). I probably would have thought, *What a bummer that that guy's car won't start*, and not stopped to see if I could help. I would have been afraid of what Richard thought of me and afraid of looking foolish, rather than stepping out to trust Jesus that he wanted to demonstrate his love for Richard by sending a random woman to pray for him and his car. I was struck that I didn't get to control the moment of what Jesus was doing, but I got to choose how I would respond to his promptings.

I had planned to trot home that day and regale my husband with a cool story about how Jesus had met me during my retreat. But Jesus had other plans for me and for Richard, who "hadn't been to church in a long time." Jesus invited me to love someone in a practical way. To trust him in feeling awkward and scared, that he wanted to do something good in me and through me by offering to pray for Richard. It didn't turn out how I had hoped and I have no idea what happened to Richard. But I do know that because of being filled with Jesus' love for me, I was able to kill the pigeon of fear and live into being a peacock of faith.

Sent Out to Love

Time and time again throughout Scripture, Jesus draws men and women into his presence and sends them out to speak and show his love to others. I may have felt like a loser earlier that day, but Jesus reminded me who I was and sent me out to bless others. He spoke through my fears, anger and inadequacies and reminded me that I don't need to be afraid to be who he made me to be. I can be a peacock because he is with me. He is guiding me. He is loving me and he is leading me. First John 4:18 says, "Such love has no fear, because perfect love expels all fear. If we are afraid, it is for fear of punishment, and this shows that we have not fully experienced his perfect love" (NLT).

You aren't going to be punished, shunned by Jesus or unloved if things go poorly when you share him with others. When we experience Jesus' love that casts out fear, it emboldens us to use our words and actions to care for others with this same kind of love. He loves you no matter what. Jesus invites us into his presence to hear his voice, experience his love, and go and tell others that he is Lord! God doesn't need more people who will do the right Christian stuff out of obligation. He wants us to be so filled with his love when we spend time with him that we are compelled to tell others about him. When we spend time with Jesus he helps us to discover who we are and how he is calling us to share our faith.

Response

What are your fears in living out and sharing your faith? Do you find yourself daydreaming about doing things that feel risky but you are scared to pursue? It could be anything—inviting a neighbor or friend over for dinner to begin building a relationship, giving time or money to a cause you've become passionate about, responding in the moment to pray for someone, caring for them in a practical way or encouraging them that Jesus loves them.

Thank Jesus that he is near to you and has chosen to send you out as his witness. Pray that Jesus would demonstrate his love for you in a powerful way and that you would have the love and boldness to tell others about it.

Rest and Other Strange Concepts

It was hard work getting out of bed and stumbling to the bathroom to get ready for church that Sunday morning. A good Christian woman goes to church every week, so I was dutiful to show up even if I felt exhausted.

A greeter asked me how I was doing as I entered the church.

"Tired," I responded.

I was on the verge of burnout after working for months to co-ordinate a campus outreach larger than had ever been done on the campus where I was serving with InterVarsity. Open-air preaching, a nationally known Christian hip-hop group, student testimonies and invitations to respond to Jesus were ramping up to a weeklong campus-wide outreach. I was overwhelmed by all the details and fell into bed exhausted every night, consumed by all the work I hadn't finished and the weight of responsibility bearing down on my sagging shoulders.

The greeter laughed and slapped me on the back. "Jesus was tired," he said. "If you're not tired, something is wrong." I wanted to punch him in his face.

Yes, even Jesus was tired. But when he was tired, he recognized he needed to eat, sleep and be restored by his Father.

We often talk about how the church should look different from the world. Sadly, though, what I see is exhausted Christian women who answer with "busy" or "stressed" when asked how they're doing and then list off all the projects, activities or errands with which they are consumed. When I read about Jesus in Scripture, I see someone taking seriously what it means to be human. Fully God and fully man, he eats, he cooks fish over hot coals for breakfast for his friends. He sleeps, sometimes curled up in the hull of a boat in the midst of storms. He plays games and laughs while religious people glare at him for spending time with messy, loud kids. He dances at parties and creates the best wine for the guests to enjoy. *The Message* translates Matthew 11:28-30 as Jesus asking, "Are you tired? Worn out? Burned out on religion? Come to me. Get away with me and you'll recover your life. I'll show you how to take a real rest. Walk with me and work with me—watch how I do it. Learn the unforced rhythms of grace. I won't lay anything heavy or ill-fitting on you. Keep company with me and you'll learn to live freely and lightly."

Bodies Matter

What if part of our witness was to demonstrate and communicate that Jesus is Lord of our bodies? Evangelism isn't simply about telling someone what they could believe. It's about living out an attractive picture of what life with Jesus is like. We need to be well rested to be attentive to his Spirit and ready to enter into his mission. Rest is a defiant act of worship in a culture that tells us we need to be more, produce more and work harder. When it comes to evangelism, the task is great: "Therefore go and make disciples of all nations" (Matthew 28:19). We need to take care of our bodies because they are the primary tools Jesus has given us to speak about and demonstrate what it means to follow him. Our inner spiritual formation has a profound impact on our outer witness. Our care for our bodies has an acute impact on our spiritual well-being.

In *The Good and Beautiful God*, James Bryan Smith writes, "Spiritual formation is the combination of our action and God's action. We must *do* something, but we rely on God to provide what is needed in order to change."[1] The same thing is true of witness. We rely on God to change us to become more aligned with his mission. We also rely on God to change the hearts of people far from him. Spiritual formation helps us to tap into that reality of the integration of our action and God's action. We can't save anyone. But we can take steps of obedience to pray, speak up and live our lives as if Jesus actually *is* Lord. We can develop our relationships with non-Christian people, serve them in practical ways and show up to be the hands and feet of Jesus in our broken world. Spiritual formation—the practices that transform us into Christ's likeness— is like the lab work we do to confirm the idea that Jesus loves us. When we go into the field we test our experiments to see if that idea is true not only for us, but for others as well. The love of Christ compels us to share him with people far from God. It becomes what we are able to give to others.

Our bodies matter to our community and they matter to God. The mission of God is tremendous, so we better be ready and rested to go where he sends us. Throughout Scripture, there are examples of this: Elijah could do nothing but sleep and eat after he defeated the prophets of Baal in 1 Kings 19:5-8; Mary sat at Jesus' feet when there was work to do to prepare for guests in Luke 10:38-42. We are people created by a God who has given us rest as a gift and as an essential part of our human experience.

> Our bodies matter to our community and they matter to God.

God has been using Psalm 23 to teach me more about rest and celebration. Psalm 23 is the classic funeral psalm—even on TV shows like *CSI*, you'll hear preachers reading this psalm. It's tempting to think that Psalm 23 only has to do with the Lord being a comforting shepherd for grieving people. However, as does the whole of Scripture, Psalm 23 is meant to point us to what our life with Jesus could be like right now and into eternity. Though this might be a familiar psalm, read it slowly a couple of times. Perhaps even insert your own name where it says "my" or "me."

> The LORD is my shepherd, I lack nothing.
>   He makes me lie down in green pastures,
> he leads me beside quiet waters,
>   he refreshes my soul.
> He guides me along the right paths
>   for his name's sake.
> Even though I walk
>   through the darkest valley,
> I will fear no evil,
>   for you are with me;
> your rod and your staff,
>   they comfort me.
> You prepare a table before me
>   in the presence of my enemies.
> You anoint my head with oil;
>   my cup overflows.
> Surely your goodness and love will follow me
>   all the days of my life,
> and I will dwell in the house of the LORD
>   forever.

That Damned Soundtrack

Psalm 23 begins with the psalmist reminding himself who the Lord is and what God offers. Perhaps he's trying to replace his mental soundtrack with the truth of who God is and how he says he'll be present for us. This psalmist is walking through death and darkness; the evil presses in around him. Yet he is telling himself that he can rest and his soul can be restored. When we are in the midst of pain and fear, it feels like we lack everything, even the basic human need of safety. By remembering and reciting the truth of who God is, the soundtrack shifts from fear to contentment and peace.

As women, we have a lot of voices in our lives and in our heads telling us what life should be like, who we should be and how we should be using our bodies. It becomes a destructive refrain that we begin to believe is true. The soundtrack in my head goes like this: *I'm so depressed about the horribly mean things this person said to me. I think I'll eat a cookie. Or take a nap. Or eat a cookie and then take a nap. I'm a loser. Nothing I do makes a difference anyway.* So I'll do those things and then I'll wake up or look at the empty glass of milk that I finished after eating the cookie and think, *Ugh, Jessica, you're such a slob. You have no self-control at all. You're trying to lose weight and be more productive and what do you do? Eat a cookie and waste time going to sleep. You really are a loser.* And then the soundtrack will say, *Tonight, I'm going to work out hardcore for at least forty-five minutes. I'll work out, and then I'll return those 300 emails that have piled up in my inbox today.* And then I make a list of ten other things I'm going to do to be self-disciplined and pro-ductive. When 9:00 p.m. rolls around, sometimes I actually do those things, but sometimes I don't. Sometimes I just watch *Parks and Recreation* or endlessly check Facebook. And that stupid soundtrack keeps playing.

Your soundtrack may not be quite the same as mine, but I'm guessing you have something similar. Maybe it's about trying to please your parents, and the soundtrack says, *If I can get on the dean's list or into med school, then my parents will love and accept me. If I could only find the right person, then I wouldn't have to be so sad and lonely and listen to One Direction in my room by myself all the time. If only I could stop this addiction in my life—cutting or porn or drugs or alcohol or massive consumer debt or perfect parenting—because I want my life to look shiny and new even though I am a mess inside . . .* The soundtrack doesn't stop.

Verse one of Psalm 23 says, "The LORD is my shepherd, I lack nothing" (or "I shall not want" in KJV). Can you imagine waking up one day and hearing and believing a soundtrack that says, *I have everything I need. I am content.* Can you imagine not staying awake worrying about having enough money, planning what you'll say in an awkward conversation with a friend or colleague, feeling the burden of parenting and all the responsibilities that go with it, criticizing yourself about your body? What if you actually believed the psalmist's words? What if these were the words we spoke to each other? I think we would all have more emotional and physical energy to share Jesus with others.

Too Tired

When we are tired, it affects everything and everyone in our lives. I was once so tired that while pulling into a gas station with my kids in the car, I accidentally nicked the side of a shiny, red Cadillac owned by an elderly black man. It was a wakeup call that, if I didn't get more sleep, I was putting my kids—and Cadillacs everywhere—in danger.

In a study done at the University of Michigan, sociologists explored the unexamined role of gender in sleep. Quoting the book *The Second Shift*, they write, "Women tend to talk more intently about being overtired, sick, and 'emotionally drained.' . . . Many women could not tear away from the topic of sleep. These women talked about sleep the way a hungry person talks about food."[2]

I have heard so many mom friends say they feel like a new woman after their baby finally sleeps for more than four hours at a time. Or female college students going home and sleeping fourteen hours straight after pulling weeks of all nighters. Or business-women who fall into their airplane seats counting on a nap to give them enough energy for the meetings they're flying to. It feels shameful to tell people that we need to sleep, because we fear we will seem weak and unproductive. We can't seem to admit that we actually need to stop and say, "I'm not a machine. I am an embodied person who needs rest."[3]

Intriguing Faith

We talk about how Christians are supposed to live out a faith that is intriguing to the rest of the world. Perhaps a good place to start is being able to trust Jesus with our finances, schedules, to-do lists, crazy kids and meetings so we can enter into the gift of rest he's designed us to need every day. Instead of talking about how tired and stressed we are, what if we began to talk about how rested and restored we were because of Jesus? What if when people asked us how we are, instead of responding "tired" or "overwhelmed," we said, "refreshed" or "content." I think a lot of people would be curious to hear why you're able to feel that way in the chaos of life.

It's been almost a decade since I began to practice the discipline of taking monthly silent retreats where I practice rest and solitude. My soul and body both begin to feel weary and anxious in a month when I forget or neglect to schedule them. Sometimes this practice comes up in conversation, but usually I try not to talk about it because when I tell people that I take daylong retreats of silence, the first thing they ask me is, "But what did you *do?*" And then they stare at me with confusion or resentment.

Non-Christian people think these retreats are cool as a day of reflection and meditation, and they're intrigued by this ancient practice of silence and solitude. I've had non-Christian friends begin to take up this practice even though they don't believe in Jesus, simply because it is so intriguing and appealing to them.

Though they don't like institutionalized religion, they'll book a couple days at a Catholic retreat center and meet with nuns who pray for them during their retreat. Many Christians, however, think it's straight-up nutso when I talk about retreats of silence. "What about your kids? Don't you have too much work to do? You mean you turn your phone *off*?!" This is inevitably followed with a look of indignation and a statement like, "Must be nice. I could never do that. I'm way too busy." Yep. Me too. And that's why I need it. To remember that God loves me for who I am, not what I can produce or how full my schedule is.

Escape or Rest?

Sleep is a tricky issue for women, and not getting enough often correlates with depression. One in five women struggles with depression.[4] As someone who has been coping for most of my life with depression through counseling, antidepressants and trying to find a healthy life balance, I know how sleep can become an escape rather than a source of rest. When I escape to bed, I don't have to deal with the real problems I have at work, in relationships, with finances or with my health. This isn't the kind of rest Jesus is talking about. This is a vicious cycle of self-loathing, anxiety and more depression.

The Mayo Clinic explored stressors that increase a woman's risk of experiencing depression, including unequal power and status because of gender, poverty and ethnicity, work overload in caring for home responsibilities as well as work responsibilities, and physical or sexual abuse.[5] All of these things produce anxiety, feelings of hopelessness and guilt. And they keep women up at night wondering how they are going to navigate unequal power systems at work, buy groceries and finish the report their boss has demanded, or work a fourteen-hour shift and study for the class they're taking to finish their degree. And they suppress the guilt and shame enough to make it through another day.

Jesus knows. He sees the chaos of our hearts, even when no one else can see. He lived in this broken, messy, dark world. His body felt tired and he took naps. He felt sad when he saw people use their bodies to harm and exploit themselves and others. I think people would be pretty excited about a God who encouraged them to nap, go to bed early and practice the Sabbath as a way of being loved by him.

The psalmist writes about rest in the midst of pain and evil because pain is something we will never escape this side of heaven. We need something, or someone, to guide us through these dark valleys. We need a caring Shepherd who knows just how exhausted we are. Jesus tells us, "Oh, honey, there is a different way. Let me show you how it's done."

Jesus Believes Your Body Matters

Our bodies matter because they are one of the tools Jesus has given us to demonstrate his love to others. Evangelism isn't just about saying the right words. It's about being present to people, being willing to spend time with them, serve them and enter their worlds. It's difficult to be present to someone when you are mentally calculating how many hours remain until you go to bed or scrambling to find a Starbucks to get some caffeine to make it through the day. Evangelism requires energy, attentiveness and a willingness to sacrifice our own agendas. When we trust Jesus with our bodies he pours into our hearts the good things from God so that we can be free to love and serve others just as God intended. When we learn to trust Jesus, we can be free to put down the things that consume us and turn instead to how he invites us to love and serve others on a daily basis.

All we have to offer others is our embodied selves. Jesus isn't just able to save our souls—Psalm 23 points to the reality that he is able to give us a rested body, a fresh mind and a restored soul. No amount of yoga, red wine or late-night TV can provide that for us. Jesus can lead us in a different way to rest to declare that he is Lord of our bodies for this exhausted broken world.

Be Quiet

Ruth Haley Barton's book *Invitation to Solitude and Silence* rocked my world when I read it during a silent retreat. Afraid that I wouldn't have enough to "do" during the retreat, I brought the book with me. Reading the chapter called "Dangerously Tired," I cried bitter tears over how angry and exhausted I was. Then I slipped into a deep, restful nap, as if Jesus himself had read me a story and tucked me in with a soft blanket and a kiss on my forehead. Barton's book is one of the primary tools Jesus used to help me learn what it means to enter into his rest so that I can be alert to his Holy Spirit, present to the people he sends me to love and filled with joy rather than bitter exhaustion.

"Perhaps the most spiritual thing we could do," Barton writes, "is get more rest so we are alert when we want to be alert." There are two kinds of tiredness: the good kind of putting in a hard day's work by expending our energy well, and the dangerous kind that I see and read about in the lives of so many women—Barton calls it "tornado tiredness." She writes,

> Dangerous tired is an atmospheric condition of the soul that is volatile and portends the risk of great destruction. It is a chronic inner fatigue accumulating over months and months, and it does not always manifest itself in physical exhaustion. In fact, it can be masked by excessive activity and compulsive overworking. When we are dangerously tired we feel out of control, compelled to constant activity.[6]

I can relate to the flurry of constant activity. I am prone to obsessively checking email and social media, reading books for professional development or doing projects. I hear that other women obsessively clean their homes. Personally, I have never struggled with this problem—my mother and the piles of dirty dishes on my kitchen counter can readily attest to that. Each of us can end up in a dangerous swirl that is harmful to ourselves and others if we aren't attentive to the brewing storm.

Barton writes that when she is dangerously tired, "I lose touch with that place in the center of my being where I know who I am in God, where I know what I am called to do, and where I am responsive to his voice above all others."[7]

That point bears repeating: *When I am tired I lose touch with who I am in God and what I am called to do.* True, there is only one of you. So you'd better take care of it.

In *The Great Omission*, Dallas Willard says, "The body is the place of our *direct* power. It is the little 'power pack' that God has assigned to us as the field of our freedom and development. Our lives depend upon our direction and management of them. . . . We . . . *must* think and plan and practice—and receive grace—if we are to succeed in doing what is right."[8]

Did you notice that Psalm 23 says, "He makes me lie down in green pastures"? God knows how poorly we treat ourselves. He knows that, unless he intervenes, we will literally run ourselves to death. My dad has always had an amazing awareness of what feeds his soul and how to lie down in green pastures—he goes hunting and fishing. It's not that he simply wants to fill his freezer with venison and fish fillets. He knows that hiking through the woods, being in solitude and enjoying nature is what feeds his soul.[9]

Move It

Sometimes rest can also look like exercise to remind us that our bodies require care and attention. Exercise can enable us to be ready for the things God has for us to do. In an article titled "The Exercise Effect," Kirsten Weir explains,

> Researchers have also explored exercise as a tool for treating—and perhaps preventing—anxiety. When we're spooked or threatened, our nervous systems jump into action, setting off a cascade of reactions such as sweating, dizziness, and a racing heart. People with heightened sensitivity to anxiety respond to those sensations with fear. They're also more likely to develop panic disorder down the road, says Jasper Smits . . . of the Anxiety Research and Treatment Program . . . in Dallas.[10]

Smits is further quoted in the article as saying, "Exercise in many ways is like exposure treatment. . . . People learn to associate the symptoms with safety instead of danger."

Think about a time when you tried to share Jesus with someone, or even *thought* about sharing Jesus with someone; you likely felt sweaty, your heart raced and you felt fear. Evangelism produces anxiety because it's scary to take a risk! Perhaps God wants to teach us through exercise that it's okay, and actually good, to feel this way—that it's a natural response to a challenge, like running a half-marathon or bringing up Jesus with your atheist brother or Muslim friend. Exercise can prepare our souls to take risks because we've experienced the victory and risk of running a half-marathon or securing the black belt in jujitsu.

As a way to take a break from the rigors of being a mom to six kids, my petite friend Emily began working out at CrossFit (yes, she's part of that cult). During the year she decided to enter a competition, trained for it and achieved a personal record of deadlifting 275 pounds! After seeing her video of her accomplishment on Facebook, I asked her what it felt like. Though she's a tough mother, she shared, "Knowing I have been able to beat personal records almost daily definitely carries over into my confidence level in other areas of life." Small steps are what put us on the path of taking on bigger challenges, physically or spiritually.

Our bodies are too important to the mission of God to live as dangerously tired women, women who harm their bodies because of eating disorders, obesity or indifference. Maybe that's why Psalm 23 is read at funerals: it's a reminder to steward our bodies while we have them, because we will all die eventually.

Sleep All Day, Party All Night . . . or Something Like That

God created us knowing our souls need to be restored through his gifts of quiet and rest. But he also gives us parties. I think this is why the psalmist provides another image to show us just how awesome life with Jesus can be.

The psalmist shifts from telling himself who God is and what he can do to directly addressing God:

> your rod and your staff,
>> they comfort me.
> You prepare a table before me
>> in the presence of my enemies.
> You anoint my head with oil. (Psalm 23:4-5)

These are all physical ways the psalmist experiences God's provision in the midst of death and darkness. God both gives us rest and lays out a party spread though the enemy and evil are ever encroaching. God marks the psalmist's head with fragrant oil to indicate he belongs to the Lord. The anointing is a tangible reminder that God cares for and is always with him . . . and with us. We all have a picture of what an awesome party is like and just how glam and stylish we'll look at that party. The psalmist knows that sometimes we need rest and other times we need to gather and celebrate in the midst of darkness and evil. God sees all the valleys we are in, the darkness we have to face every day. He knows we want to slink into a hole to be depressed, or cry our eyes out, or punch somebody because we are in so much pain. And he says, "You know what would be awesome? A party."

The kind of party the psalmist is advocating for and the kind of party other people throw might look the same, but the motivations are totally different. We've all been to parties where it is clear that the host is doing everything to impress the guests, show off and flaunt how much money they spent on the celebration. Gross. Other parties are so pathetic that they look more like a mandatory office meeting—an open bag of chips and a few two-liters of lukewarm soda do not a party make. It's clear the host either hasn't put much effort into it or doesn't care enough for the guests to provide anything better. Double gross.

I want you to picture a long banquet table with all your favorite foods. It's set beautifully with twinkling crystal glasses, delicate yellow flowers in slender vases and fine china set on crisp white linens. Candles glow and create an inviting ambiance. There are all the comfort foods at the top of your list. God says, "Come, I have it all ready for you." God's motivation for throwing a party is a defiant act of celebration and love in the midst of fear and encroaching enemies. An act of love only an all-powerful Creator could provide. Do you remember what it was like when your mom or another family member made your favorite food when you were little? It was always a special night when my mom made chicken and dumplings on bitterly cold nights in Michigan's Upper Peninsula. You'd come to the table so excited to dig in, feeling incredibly loved that she would do something special for you. And you'd sit there, legs swinging in the chair, delighting in the yumminess of what was before you. You weren't thinking about the calories you'd have to burn off later or how you'd eat a salad to compensate for the calories you were consuming. You were simply lost in the delight of being cared for and loved during a meal.

And just like a child, Jesus rests at the table, grinning from ear to ear seeing you and your community enjoy the table he's set before you. He leans in with his chin resting in one hand, elbow propped on the table, and encourages you, "Tell me more about your day. Oh, I'd love to hear that story again. I love hearing your laugh." And with the other arm, he's holding back the darkness. The glint of sword blades and arrow tips are there in the darkness—glaring eyes, hateful hearts pressing in all around the table, enemies seeking to rob you of the contentment, security and joy of that moment—but Jesus holds them back. There, at the table with him, you lack nothing. Nothing.

Rachel Marie Stone writes in *Eat with Joy,*

> It's no accident that praying before eating is often called "saying grace." . . . The words we use to talk about food and bodies matter . . . because they nourish and shape and feed us—or poison, warp and starve us—every bit as much as food does. Who can eat gratefully and joyfully while thinking, *I'm an ugly pig who doesn't deserve to eat?* I couldn't. Who can eat with real pleasure when the table talk centers on dimply thighs, flabby bellies, calories, cholesterol and what's "healthy" or "unhealthy"? No one can, and such talk actually fuels disorder in the form of *over*eating at least as much as it fuels disorder in the form of *under*eating.[11]

Jesus—the one who created food and who loved to party when he walked the earth—says there will be a big party when he returns and you will worship God together forever. You'll be given a new body that will never get tired, never be harmed, never have to go through guilt-driven fitness regimens. You will be content because he is your Shepherd and has given you everything you need.

Jesus Demonstrates the Spiritual with the Physical

Sleeping and eating—Jesus gave us these gifts as a way to restore our soul, yet they are the most abused and disturbed areas of women's lives. He uses bodies, sleep, food and parties to show us that our physical world matters. In Scripture, there are many examples of the ways Jesus uses physical things to signify spiritual realities. Even in Psalm 23 we read about lying down in a pasture, walking beside quiet waters, pulling a chair up to a lavishly spread table and feeling anointing oil drip down a forehead.

Carried Away

When my husband and I were preparing to move from Grand Rapids to Cleveland, I felt anxious about finding a house, selling ours, writing papers for grad school and packing up a house while caring for our three-year-old son. I developed a tic in one of my eyes from how much stress I felt.

There was a stream near our home that I would run by. A small bridge went over it and continued onto the running trail. One autumn day as I stopped to catch my breath, I watched the golden, crimson and amber leaves drift down the river. I picked up one of the leaves and silently said a prayer about one of the things I was worried about, then sent it with the leaf floating down the river. Then, I sent twenty or more leaves drifting down the cool waters. I watched them swirl around in pools or get caught in branches protruding from the bank. With each leaf I sent adrift, I felt the burden lift from my shoulders as I physically experienced what Jesus was doing spiritually.

We need to be active in experiencing the presence of the Holy Spirit so that we can bring his peace into every interaction we have. The great evangelist of the 1800s Charles Spurgeon wrote,

> A vigorous Christian's life consists in gracious activity. We not only think, but we act. We are not always lying down to feed, but are journeying onward toward perfection; hence we read,

"he leadeth me beside the still waters." What are these "still waters" but the influences and graces of his blessed Spirit? His Spirit attends us in various operations, like waters—in the plural— to cleanse, to refresh, to fertilise, to cherish. They are *"still waters,"* for the Holy Ghost loves peace, and sounds no trumpet of ostentation in his operations. He may flow into our soul, but not into our neighbour's, and therefore our neighbour may not perceive the divine presence; and though the blessed Spirit may be pouring his floods into one heart, yet he that sitteth next to the favoured one may know nothing of it.[12]

Flooding our hearts, the love of Jesus influences us to love others. The neighbor next door, the foster child, the ignored elderly person, the pompous businessman or businesswoman. The still waters we experience begin to seep into every area of life, rivulets of grace extending to others who are dying of thirst. Imagine what God would do through people who trust him to care for their bodies. Imagine the powerful message it would communicate to people far from God: I can rest because I lack nothing when I trust Jesus to lead me and provide for me.

Imagine sharing stories with non-Christian friends and family members about how that's happened in your life. I think it would leave them with a taste of something good that only God can offer. Jesus wants to use our bodies to demonstrate to others that he is Lord.

Response

I want you to do something active. If you live in a place where you can take a walk by a stream, a lake or some other body of water, make time to go. Actually go and walk beside quiet waters. Once you get there, find leaves, stones or some other item that you can throw into the water. As you throw stones or let leaves float away, send each one with a prayer of what you are anxious about. It might be a friend or family member whom you long to know Jesus, an area of sin or brokenness in your life or fears you are holding onto. Jesus wants to lead you beside quiet waters to restore your soul. Part of that involves your trusting him with what troubles your soul.

If you're not physically able to get to a place like this, your imagination is the perfect destination. The Holy Spirit is able to give you meaningful pictures that can powerfully cement God's work in your life. Use a journal to write about or draw a picture of what this would look like. In your mind, picture a place with quiet waters that you enjoy, a place that is personally restful. Picture a comfortable spot and settle down next to this body of water. Imagine what you would touch, whether it is sand, pebbles or acorns. Feel the sunlight on your face and smell the scents of God's created goodness around you. Picture yourself picking up a rock, holding it in the palm of your hand and casting your anxieties onto it. See yourself throwing it into the body of water and prayerfully trusting Jesus that he is able to take your burdens. Do this for each of the things about which you are anxious and burdened. Take a deep breath. Thank Jesus that he is the one who is able to restore your soul and lead you down the right paths so that he'll be glorified.

Life Changes, God Is Unchanging

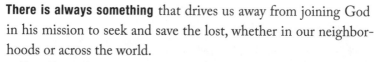

There is always something that drives us away from joining God in his mission to seek and save the lost, whether in our neighborhoods or across the world.

In college, it's obsessing about the boy down the hall or pulling an all nighter to finish writing a paper on Greek mythology. After college, it's stressing about getting the right job, becoming independent and, dang it, not being able to eat like a college student anymore. If you get engaged, you obsess about the perfect wedding and what life will be like with your husband. If you remain single when all of your friends seem to be getting married, you obsess about whether to find a better job or start online dating. If you're married, it's whether to have kids and how many, when to enroll them in soccer, gymnastics or Chinese language immersion. Then it's about paying for braces, college, hoping your sons don't get addicted to porn and your daughters will have a healthy body image (or vice versa). Soon you're entering retirement, obsessing about who is taking cooler vacations, how accomplished your kids or grandkids are, whether you've achieved enough at this point in your life, or who looks far younger than her age ("Did she have work done? I swear it's Botox!"). And then, and then, and then . . . It never ends.

The problem is that "and then" doesn't change no matter our stage of life. No matter how old we are, we are meant to join Jesus in his mission to speak about and demonstrate his love to others. Jesus' command to "go and make disciples" (Matthew 28:19) doesn't have provisos or caveats to it like, "go and make disciples when you're _____." There is only a command: "go and make disciples of all nations." And when we stand before Jesus someday, I don't think he's going to tell any of us, "Oh, you? Yeah, your life was craaaaaazy when you were in grad school. You get a pass for not telling people about me." As long as we live, no matter what our age or what is going on in our lives, Jesus issues his command: "go and make disciples of all nations."

Young Girls and Old Women

When my husband and I were looking for our first home, we toured a lot of houses in our limited price range. At one of the Sunday open houses, the family was home and had put out a plate of cookies to welcome prospective buyers to their cozy bungalow. Their precocious five-year-old daughter chatted us up about how she liked the big backyard and how her church was nearby.

"Do you know Jesus?" she asked as she munched a cookie. "I love learning about him in Sunday school!"

Her parents looked embarrassed by their daughter's boldness and glanced at us nervously to see how we would respond.

I smiled. "Yes, I do love Jesus too! Isn't it amazing how he does so many cool things?"

She nodded with enthusiasm and ran off to give her mom a hug.

The parents apologized for their daughter, but I loved seeing this little girl's boldness. What she was learning at church made her excited about Jesus and excited to tell others about him. She didn't have any fears that we would launch into intellectual objections about Jesus. She just loved Jesus and wanted to tell me about him.

In Matthew 19:14 Jesus rebukes the disciples when they try to shoo the excited and messy kids away from him one warm afternoon. The disciples think Jesus should attend to the important work of teaching adults or solemnly praying about the sinners they have been meeting. Yet Jesus tells them, "Let the children come to me. Don't stop them! For the Kingdom of Heaven belongs to those who are like these children" (NLT). Children come to Jesus with full and open hearts and leave his presence with full and open hearts to share him with others. The kingdom of heaven belongs to people with hearts that love and trust Jesus like children. There is nothing to hold kids back from sharing Jesus because all they've known is that Jesus is awesome and he loves them.

Years later I knelt down next to the chair in which an elderly woman was sitting, her walker pushed to the side of the room in the church basement where I was leading evangelism training. Hazel, in her polyester suit jacket with flowered brooch, reminded me of my own grandmother who had passed away just a few months earlier.

"Mother wanted to come to the training today to learn how to share the gospel," her daughter explained. "She's ninety-three."

"In my retirement home," Hazel shared, "there are people who don't know Jesus. I want to tell them, because who else will?" I was intrigued. What was it about Hazel's life that she could be so aligned with Jesus' mission in her twilight years? I wondered if she had been like this her whole life, and how she had managed to stay missional through decades of change.

The similarity of the precocious little girl and the bold elderly woman is convicting. For me and so many others, the zeal for sharing Jesus always seems to wane under the pressures of choosing a major, finding a job or worrying about offending colleagues or friends. Or being immobilized in fear of looking stupid, not having the right answers or seeming like an aggressive fundamentalist weirdo. In recalling my experiences with Hazel and with the little girl, I was struck by the truth of Hebrews 13:8: "Jesus Christ is the same yesterday and today and forever." Our lives may change, but Jesus continuously invites us to participate in his mission to seek and save the lost until his triumphant return. No matter how old or young we are, our circumstances don't limit how God can use us. We need to keep asking Jesus, "Who have you sent me to share your good news with at this stage in life?"

Check Yourself Before You Wreck Yourself

Evangelism is one of the most difficult spiritual disciplines to consistently practice. It forces us to depend on God instead of ourselves, to put our words and deeds into action, and to willingly and compassionately engage with people whose beliefs are different from ours. Our faith can easily turn inward, and in a consumerist Christian culture that talks about "getting fed" and "being spiritually filled," it's hard to reject the idea that our faith is only for ourselves. The message we get in culture and in church is often the same: it's about you and your needs.

But in the timeless words of the rapper Ice Cube, "You better check yo'self before you wreck yo'self." Individually and corporately, we need to heed Ice Cube's words—or better yet, Jesus' words in Matthew 5:13-16.

> You are the salt of the earth. But if the salt loses its saltiness, how can it be made salty again? It is no longer good for anything, except to be thrown out and trampled underfoot.
>
> You are the light of the world. A town built on a hill cannot be hidden. Neither do people light a lamp and put it under a bowl. Instead they put it on its stand, and it gives light to everyone in the house. In the same way, let your light shine

before others, that they may see your good deeds and glorify your Father in heaven.

Salt that isn't salty gets thrown out and trampled on. What does that mean for evangelism? I think it means that when we choose not to engage in Jesus' mission and be salty folks, we throw away our lives, we throw away our purpose, and we get trampled on. We forget what life is meant to be and become consumed with our own agendas instead of God's mission. Some people do intentionally hide their light under a bushel because they're embarrassed or they're worried it will cost them their job, life or family.

> When we choose not to engage in Jesus' mission and be salty folks, we throw away our lives, we throw away our purpose, and we get trampled on.

Hiding our light not only prevents others from seeing more of Jesus, but it's also just dumb and contrary to what lights are meant to do. Lights are meant to shine. Salt is meant to be salty. Followers of Jesus are meant to be some dazzling, savory folk.

We need to check ourselves before we wreck ourselves. Life isn't about getting what we want and fulfilling our desires. It's about God's purposes for us and for the world, and because he loves us so much he gives us a greater desire for what he wants.

> Followers of Jesus are meant to be some dazzling, savory folk.

Sin Sickness

Our faith becomes a train wreck when we make it about ourselves. Scripture demonstrates that religion—personal or structural—can become sinful. Sin isn't just the stuff we do that offends God. It's the rebellious spirit inside us that constantly demands the focus of life to be on ourselves. We try to manipulate our worlds to revolve around our desires, priorities and fears, and demand in small or large ways that the people around us acquiesce to what we think life should be like. Sin is a disease where we choose our own ways instead of God's ways. And we sin at every stage of life.

We gossip about others because we want to avoid the pain and ugliness in our own lives. We endlessly work out because we believe worth is found in a well-sculpted butt. We fill our online shopping carts with items to distract ourselves from the pain of disappointment, fear and resentment. We escape into sexual fantasies in thought or deed, which Jesus teaches are the same. We work hard in our careers or academics because we believe we need to prove we're smart and successful in order to feel better about ourselves. We get crusty and bitter because of all the ways we have been marginalized as women, and our hearts grow hard toward Jesus, his church and others. We sink into self-pity and depression because we believe we are nobody and nothing to God or anyone else.

Many of these areas aren't even addressed from the pulpit or in small groups. The church is just now feeling bold enough to address that men are addicted to porn, so the women sit and silently struggle with areas of sin and brokenness. There seem to be no solutions for dealing with lust, materialism, perfectionism or abuse. And evangelism feels like one more expectation to be a perfect Christian woman when already most of us feel like failures because it's been a while since we've prayed more than a quick prayer of "Help!" or spent time in Scripture beyond the Sunday sermon.

I Want a Perfect Body, I Want a Perfect Soul

I could fill this book with all the gross, disgusting, rebellious ways I put myself first and choose my way instead of God's way on a daily basis. How insanely jealous I get when I see a friend taking yet another vacation with her husband to Europe when Dave and I are trying to make ten dollars stretch to eat gourmet hot dogs in Cleveland. I effortlessly make an idol out of my desires, priorities and even religious deeds, and I burn myself out trying to be perfect. And then I get angry with God, others and myself.

Without something drastic done to heal us of our soul sickness, we spend our days seeking after things that won't satisfy us and perpetuating the cycle of pain, death and brokenness in our lives, relationships and world. Tim Keller writes, "Idols distort not only our thinking but also our feelings."[1] For women, this affects how we view ourselves, others and God. Our thoughts or feelings consume us and we forget that Jesus is the one who is able to guide us into love, peace and joy. Part of how God does that in our lives is through our sharing his love with others who are far from him.

The Antidote

The amazing thing about evangelism is that it becomes an antidote to consumerist faith and self-focus at every stage of life. Lisa, a college student in Texas, was stressed about completing a huge paper for her sociology class. But her friend began to share with her about how depressed she was that her boyfriend broke up with her and that she felt far from God, and Lisa realized that Jesus was inviting her to pause from her own stress and share Jesus' love with her hurting friend.

Debbie, a retired woman I met a few years ago, shared with me about how she remembers being so exhausted one day after dropping her sons off at school, and she went to McDonald's to relax with a cup of coffee and have a quiet time. She told me,

> As I turned from the counter with coffee in hand, someone bumped me so I spilled my coffee on a woman sitting with twin toddlers. As I helped her sop up the coffee, she was crying and I thought my coffee had burned her. She said no, and explained, "My mother-in-law is dying of cancer, and these children love her—how do I explain this to them?" I

said, "Well it kind of depends on what you think happens after you die—do you have a sense of that?" She asked me to sit, and explained that she was a "lapsed Catholic," unsure of what she believed anymore. I asked if she'd like to meet at that McDonald's again to go through One to One (an old weekly investigative Bible study I've used countless times since I first saw it in 1978). She readily agreed and we met at that same place, with her kids in their high chairs, every Tuesday during my kids' preschool hour for the next six weeks.

Debbie had gone to McDonald's to spend time growing her spiritual life. But she realized that part of growing her spiritual life was sharing Jesus with others! Instead of exploring Jesus on her own, Debbie got to explore Jesus with someone who wasn't familiar with him. It fueled her prayer life, her dependency on God and her desire to understand the Scriptures better. It tuned her into the reality that following Jesus isn't just about learning more—it's about actively responding to the Holy Spirit's promptings and being obedient to follow him.

As we share about Jesus' sacrifice, we remember what really matters in life and in our own faith. We become grateful that he saved us despite all the brokenness in our lives and ugliness of our souls. We continue to repent from our sin and trust more in the Holy Spirit as he leads us into greater sanctification. The gospel isn't just good news for others. It's good news for us. Through evangelism we learn how to apply the gospel message to our own lives even as we help others learn how to do the same.

> Through evangelism we learn how to apply the gospel message to our own lives even as we help others learn how to do the same.

As a young campus minister I struggled with the weight of caring for broken college students in the midst of dealing with my own pain and sinful choices. There were mornings I lay in bed, depressed and immobilized at my inability to lead and love others well. I would force myself to get out of bed, take a shower and drive to campus to meet with students. Some of those days I had scheduled to teach students how to share their faith—and it was the last thing I felt like doing. I felt alone, insecure and far from God. Prayer felt hollow, and I wouldn't have shared Jesus with anyone that day had it not been in my job description to do so. Students were typically scared to strike up spiritual conversations with others, and I could have easily changed the agenda to study Scripture, take a prayer walk or talk about their areas of brokenness and stress (a topic any college student can talk about for a very. long. time.). I would drive home at night through what I called "the gauntlet," a row of fast-food restaurants that I would inevitably stop at to buy a bag of greasy, salty food to console myself with after a long day. In the mornings I would wake up thirsty and bloated. I gained a bunch of weight from these late-night binges, and I became frustrated and angry in addition to being depressed. I felt sluggish, chubby and ashamed of my choices, yet I couldn't seem to stop this bad habit.

Even in the midst of this, each time I stepped out in faith to share Jesus, something profound happened. I would see the Holy Spirit working in the lives of my student and the person we were sharing Jesus with, and I would feel my own hard and bitter heart start to soften. Students became Christians when we shared the gospel! My Christian students were shocked and excited when they saw that the gospel was powerful. When we stepped out in faith we experienced how God was moving in the lives of their friends, and even strangers. It made us pray like crazy, excited to talk to more people about Jesus and expectant of the ways God would continue to show up. So many days I wouldn't feel like sharing Jesus, but by acting and responding in faith, I found that he was always there. It was me who needed to show up and join Jesus where he was already at work.

Evangelism isn't about us, but God amazingly uses it to heal us of our sin and ways we've pushed him away. As we share Jesus, our heart blossoms in love for him time and time again as we remember just how good the good news is. We become more content with who we are and what we have because we realize that Jesus is enough. We see again that Jesus is all that matters—not our traditions, denominations or rituals. Jesus is the one who can heal us from the inside out to go and be an agent of healing and love in his world. Ironically, it is often when we feel least prepared, least worshipful and least confident that Jesus shows up, just like he has for me time and time again, to remind us that he is Lord and we are not.

The Great Cloud of Sisters

We will always have hardship, sin and pain. We will always struggle with idols crowding out the place in our lives that was meant for God. It is likely that you won't feel excited to tell others about Jesus when you hop out of bed in the morning. We can let our thoughts and feelings stop us or we can remember we are surrounded by women and men who have chosen to worship and proclaim Jesus despite their suffering or fear. We need each other to remember that Jesus has created us to share his good news. We need each other to remember God's promise in life and in evangelism: "He will never leave you nor forsake you" (Deuteronomy 31:6).

When we feel like he has forgotten us, we can dig a little in church history to read the stories of fearless, bold and loving women like Saint Hildegard of Bingen, the Benedictine mystic in the 1100s who composed poetry, music and volumes of theology as she served as a doctor in her monastery. Hildegard was sickly from birth, and when she believed God was inviting her to write down the visions she had been experiencing her whole life, she became physically ill. In her first theological text, Hildegard wrote about her internal struggle, pain and fear in recording what she was experiencing in Scripture. "While I was doing it, I sensed, as I mentioned before, the deep profundity of scriptural exposition; and, raising myself from illness by the strength I received, I brought this work to a close—though just barely—in ten years. . . . And I spoke and wrote these things not by the invention of my heart or that of any other person, but as by the secret mysteries of God I heard and received them in the heavenly places."[2] Hildegard was sick and afraid, yet she received strength from God to finish the work she had been called to do.

Jarena Lee, a black woman who lived in the 1800s, traveled over 2,000 miles on foot to preach the gospel from town to town. Lee faced hostility wherever she went because of her ethnicity and gender, but the Holy Spirit empowered her to preach. "Go preach the gospel! Preach the gospel! I will put words in your mouth!" he seemed to say. Though she was barred from preaching in the Methodist church, she continued to do so out of her love and obedience to Jesus. God worked through her perseverance and led the African Methodist Episcopal Church leaders to authorize and bless her work as a preacher.[3]

Aimee Semple McPherson, a prolific evangelist in the 1920s, preached across the United States, often nailing in the tent stakes for the tents where she preached at night for evangelistic revival. Her story is fascinating, miraculous and sorrowful. Stranded in China with a newborn baby after her husband died in their work as missionaries, she returned to the United States and married again. Though she tried to be content as a mother and housewife, she suffered from depression and several botched operations after the birth of her son, Rolf. Over time, Aimee heeded the Lord's call despite her fear of traveling with young children to preach and essentially live in poverty. Her preaching ministry grew to such prominence that she reached groups as diverse as Gypsy tribes, the

Ku Klux Klan, prominent US senators and poverty-stricken black workers in the cotton and tobacco fields of the South with the gospel. She pioneered religious radio broadcasting and mobilized her church to care for millions of people during the Great Depression. Her story ends tragically, but as with many people in Scripture (like King David), her life points to the struggle to obey God in the midst of fear, bucking societal norms and terrible moral failures.[4]

The stories of these women have been a comfort to me. These were ordinary women who simply said yes to God. Carolyn Custis James has written a wonderful book called *Lost Women of the Bible* that explores the stories of brave women throughout the Old and New Testaments. Michelle DeRusha has a recent book called *50 Women Every Christian Should Know*, which I promptly ordered upon discovering it! Reading the stories of women in Scripture and in history helps me to put my life in perspective. The problems I struggle with are small in comparison with what these women faced. And it helps to know they weren't perfect either—they still struggled, sinned and screwed up bigtime.

These sisters are reminders that we are part of a "great cloud of witnesses," as Hebrews 12 says. Sometimes I imagine them hanging out together, cheering me on to be bold. I picture Hildegard, Jarena and Aimee smiling on me from heaven, nudging each other and saying, "Go 'head, girl! Jesus is sending you out! Do the work of an evangelist!" It can be tempting to put historical Christian women on a platform, but all they did was continue to say yes to Jesus and his mission despite the barriers they faced internally or externally. They kept saying yes to Jesus, they kept coming back to him to be filled with love and they did so throughout so many different life stages—as young girls and old women, as mothers, nuns and wives. So diverse, yet each faithful to proclaim Jesus. No matter what changes in life, it is freeing to realize that Jesus remains the same yesterday, today and forever. His call to join him in mission isn't based on our age, ethnicity, work life, home life, marital status or gender. His call to make disciples remains the same yesterday, today and until he returns to judge the living and the dead.

In her book *Wonder Women*, author Kate Harris writes about the challenge of compartmentalizing our lives: "Vocation today is often understood in terms of a job or career, but historically it meant much more than that. When we understand its deeper significance, we find a meaningful and consistent framework to help us think about our multiple life commitments."[5]

We like to compartmentalize our lives, but all of us manage multiple life commitments; we are simultaneously some combination of sister, student, wife, employee, friend or caregiver. Most importantly we are women who are followers of Jesus sent to love others who are far from God in every area of our lives. We are to blaze with the love of Jesus, whether crippled in a hospital bed, living on a college campus or leading meetings in the boardroom.

Jesus has enough love for you and the people in your life who don't yet know him. He will be faithful to fill you with his love as you take a risk to speak about and demonstrate his love no matter what life stage you're in and how you're struggling. We need more women to love others by sharing Jesus until he takes us home. We need to step out and believe that evangelism doesn't rest on our shoulders—we can be empowered by, through and for Jesus through his ever-present Holy Spirit. We just need to say yes, and like with Jarena Lee, he will give us the words to speak.

Jesus is moving in the lives of people around us. We just have to show up and be willing to speak about and demonstrate his love to others. Though it can feel scary to engage in this lifelong mission, we are meant to do so in community—with Jesus and the women and men who are his presence here on earth—mindful of the legacy of the great cloud of sisters we are part of.

Response

Faith is about trusting Jesus with what you have at the stage of life you're in. Ask Jesus to help you identify the barriers you face in this current life stage. Ask him to help you identify the strategic witness you currently have. Write down one small action step you can take to speak about or demonstrate Christ's love to someone in your life.

Spend some time confessing sins of selfishness, self-protection and resentment. Pray that Jesus would renew your faith and grow your love for him and his people.

Compassionate Calluses

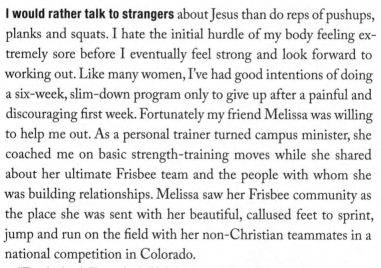

I would rather talk to strangers about Jesus than do reps of pushups, planks and squats. I hate the initial hurdle of my body feeling extremely sore before I eventually feel strong and look forward to working out. Like many women, I've had good intentions of doing a six-week, slim-down program only to give up after a painful and discouraging first week. Fortunately my friend Melissa was willing to help me out. As a personal trainer turned campus minister, she coached me on basic strength-training moves while she shared about her ultimate Frisbee team and the people with whom she was building relationships. Melissa saw her Frisbee community as the place she was sent with her beautiful, callused feet to sprint, jump and run on the field with her non-Christian teammates in a national competition in Colorado.

"Don't think I'm a dork," Melissa said, "but I'm going to measure out 100 yards to do some sprints to be ready for when my team gets back together."

Dork was the last word I would have used to describe her. *Beast, warrior* or *hardcore* were the words that came to mind for my friend whose twinkly blue eyes grew intensely focused when she was competing in a pickup game of volleyball or getting ready for an ultimate Frisbee tournament.

I mentioned how I was looking forward to getting a pedicure after our month in the wilderness of Michigan's Upper Peninsula, and I asked her if she'd be doing the same to pamper her tootsies.

"No way!" she shook her head, eyes widening at the suggestion of such a spa treatment. "I need my calluses! I had a pedicure done once. The woman cut off all my calluses. When I went to play ultimate Frisbee with my team, I put on my cleats and *owwwwww*!"

We had begun to do our pushups. While I was trying to concentrate on my breathing, she went on about the dastardly nail tech who ruined her perfectly callused feet.

"Without the calluses," she said, "all the time of training my feet to be prepared for our games was gone. My feet hurt so badly until I developed the calluses again."

We normally think of calluses as a negative or ugly thing, something to get rid of and slough away. However, for Melissa, her calloused feet are exactly what she needs to do something she enjoys. They enable her to make a meaningful contribution to her ultimate Frisbee team and stay in the game. Activities like playing the guitar, dancing ballet and pounding a hammer all feel awkward and painful until calluses develop. Once we become proficient and have developed calluses, we're quick to engage in these things because we know the reward is great and the discomfort becomes minimal.

We need to keep engaging in the activity so that we don't lose what we've gained and have to go through the painful process of developing calluses all over again. Evangelism is much the same way—we need to persevere in sharing our faith even when it's painful, awkward and disappointing. It's the perseverance that helps us get to the place of enjoying talking about Jesus rather than dreading it. Evangelism requires using parts of our faith and souls that many of us aren't accustomed to using. Like starting a new exercise routine or learning how to play the guitar, the first attempts can make us want to give up and never try again.

Jesus knew the sting of disappointment, fear and rejection. Being fully human, Jesus felt the depths of pain when he was rejected. But he kept going because he knew the reward was greater than the cost. He ran away from cities to escape people who wanted to stone him to death for proclaiming the kingdom of God. He sat down with throbbing feet at the end of a long day of standing and preaching parables to the crowds, knowing that many would reject his words. Jesus and his beautiful callused feet are the model for persevering in the midst of rejection, fear and pain.

The author of Hebrews writes,

> Therefore, since we are surrounded by such a great cloud of witnesses, let us throw off everything that hinders and the sin that so easily entangles. And let us run with perseverance the race marked out for us, fixing our eyes on Jesus, the pioneer and perfecter of faith. For the joy set before him he endured the cross, scorning its shame, and sat down at the right hand of the throne of God. Consider him who endured such opposition from sinners, so that you will not grow weary and lose heart. (Hebrews 12:1-3)

This is one of my favorite passages. I love how these verses remind us that we are not alone. The language is plural: "we," "us," "our." We are surrounded by a great cloud of witnesses, both from the past and around us right now. We aren't meant to run this race alone. God has given us a community to help us get up and keep running when we are discouraged, not because that's what a good Christian woman does, but for the *joy* set before us. People are God's greatest treasure, and there are examples all throughout Scripture of Jesus enjoying the company of the people he was with, laughing with little children, relaxing and drinking wine at a party, and talking with the disciples as they walked from town to town.

The people in your life are God's greatest treasure too. And, like my friend Melissa, you are meant to love and serve them in what you already enjoy doing. It can be too easy to insulate ourselves with Christians and make every activity in life focused on the church. But Jesus didn't say, "Focus on serving the church." He said, "Feed my sheep" (John 21:17) because the sheep are lost.

Think about some of the activities you like doing. What are ways you can begin to do life with non-Christians to demonstrate what it means to love and follow Jesus? What if your book club made it a point to invite non-Christian friends, pray for them regularly and take risks to share Jesus together? What if you joined a club volleyball team or gamer guild on your campus with another Christian with the intention of praying for and reaching out to a community with whom you shared similar interests? We can encourage each other to stay in the race when it gets rough while we're actually doing something we enjoy.

Entangled

We will get tripped up in witness. Situations hinder us and sins entangle. Evangelism is one of those things that we easily drop because we don't see the immediate benefit to ourselves. And since we're selfish people, we need God to continually reorient our hearts to loving others.

I get entangled with sin when I overbook my schedule, waste hours on Facebook instead of interacting with the real live people in my neighborhood, and resent it when someone actually wants to talk about Jesus when I'm too tired and busy. We're hindered when we try to engage in witness alone and muster up the courage to share Jesus. Pretty soon we convince ourselves that it will be too embarrassing, costly and weird and that no one really wants to hear about Jesus anyway. We need each other to help us get untangled from things that detract us from witness. We need our churches, our small groups and girlfriends to remind us of what is important:

there are women and men wasting away in spiritual and physical death whom we are sent to love.

Look at your schedule. What do you spend time on? Make a list of everything that consumes your time. We're all busy, but if I'm honest, I could have taken a half hour to talk

> We need each other to help us get untangled from things that detract us from witness.

with my neighbor while outside gardening instead of perusing modcloth.com for clothing I'm not actually going to buy. There are also things I can invite others to do with me that I'm going to do anyway. I need to eat every day, and I could easily make a little more and invite the retired couple who live down the street or the families who do Cub Scouts with my son. Ideally, I should exercise every day, and there are people I could invite to take a walk or go to a Zumba class.

In addition to thinking about spending time with non-Christian friends, who are Christian friends with whom you can commit to pursue witness together this year? To encourage each other, my friend Amy committed to talk, pray and have a private blog with another friend. They call their blog *Successful Surrender* to remind themselves that taking risks to follow Jesus and share him with others is about dying to self on a daily basis.

Choosing to share Jesus doesn't need to be complicated. You can set up calendar reminders on your phone or computer to pray for or connect with someone. Getting together in person or on the phone with another Christian to check in on how your witness is going can be enough. Just like we need fitness buddies to hold us accountable, we need witness buddies to hold us accountable to speak and live out Jesus to others far from God.

Run the Race

Like fitness regimens, it can be confusing, overwhelming and scary to figure out where to start sharing your faith with others. In my workouts, I've benefited from programs like Couch to 5k that help me start slowly so that I don't burn out and am more likely to keep running. I've got a voice command on the app that tells me when to run and walk, when to push harder, and when to slow down. The Holy Spirit does the same for us as we take risks to share Jesus. He serves as the guide who prompts us to slow down with friends who are skeptical about Jesus and have been hurt by the church. He reminds us when to kick it into high gear and take risks that push us to share the gospel even when we're scared to do it.

I can typically tell when the Holy Spirit is prompting me to do something risky because my heart starts to beat faster, I get sweaty and begin to list all the reasons that what I'm feeling compelled to do isn't logical, is too weird or is unnecessary. He often gives us physical indications of his presence so that we realize it's time to take a risk!

Just like we don't go from being sedentary to running a marathon overnight, no one is asking you to do open-air preaching in the middle of Times Square to start sharing your faith. Pick something that feels like a reasonable risk and tell a friend about it so that she or he can pray for you and encourage you in reaching out to others.

To remind himself to run the race with perseverance, my friend Dan posted a Bible verse on his computer to encourage him throughout the day. His colleague Tia noticed it and it sparked a conversation about his beliefs. To Dan's surprise, she actually liked the verse so much she snatched it from his desk and posted it on her own! Now she comes back to talk with him every day to see if he has a new Bible verse posted on his computer. He finally gave her a Bible so that she would stop stealing his Post-it notes.

Develop your faith muscles and calluses in sharing Jesus. Katty

Kay and Claire Shipman, in their groundbreaking book *The Confidence Code*, explore how women develop confidence. Contrary to the principle most of us have been told—to "fake it till you make it"—Kay and Shipman encourage women to "fail fast."[1] Instead of obsessing about how to do things perfectly or waiting until the ideal moment, doing something and failing shows us that the world isn't going to end if someone turns us down for a date or isn't into an idea we've presented at work. The same thing is true of evangelism—fail fast. Recognize that Jesus still loves you, your friendship is still intact and you aren't going to get fired at work if you invite someone to church.

If it feels too intimidating to do this with evangelism, start with something else. My friend Leslie took a risk in starting her own consulting business—a scary step in moving away from the consistent income of working with a consulting firm. Early on she made mistakes in organizing her time and overcommitted herself, missing a couple coaching calls. She began to worry that she wouldn't be able to balance family life and her work and spent some time crying with her husband and mentor, worried she had made a mistake. But she kept going, persevering until she found an eventual groove that worked well for her clients and her kids. Though it was difficult at first, the failures prompted Leslie to keep at it to find something that worked for her rather than walk away and quit.

The more you fail, the more you begin to realize that failure is part of the process of developing confidence. Failure helps us to see that often it's not about getting things perfect—it's about persevering in reaching a goal.

Endure Opposition

Most of us are pain averse; we do everything in our power to avoid things that will cause us to feel weak, incompetent, scared or powerless. But frankly, all of us come to the table this way when it comes to sharing our faith. We can't muster up power or skill on our own. When we share Jesus, we will encounter opposition, but we have the choice to endure it or escape it. You will feel stupid, not know all the answers, be rejected by some people and realize very quickly that you can't save anyone no matter how much you'd like to.

Spiritual forces are working to prevent us from sharing Jesus, to stop us in our tracks and shut our mouths. The last thing Satan wants to see is an army of women boldly and lovingly sharing the gospel, serving others and looking to Jesus as their hope. It is scary thinking about people rejecting you, making you look foolish or making you stick out as the lone Christian in your neighborhood, dorm or office. For women, the possibility of hurting relationships because of our faith is one of the scariest things. We don't want to offend others or feel like we've failed a friend.

I regularly prayed for my friend Gia, who grew up as a pastor's kid but walked away from her faith, disgusted by the fundamentalist legalism she experienced growing up. We decided to get together a couple days a week to do yoga in her basement and then eat breakfast together. Knowing she had been really hurt by the church and was leery of anyone trying to talk to her about Christianity, I prayed a lot before broaching the subject of Jesus with her. Rather than inviting her to church, which I knew would likely be uncomfortable for her, I invited her to do an investigative Bible study with me. I told her we could look at Scripture to see what Jesus said for himself rather than believing what her fundamentalist father had drilled into her.

"Don't try to save me," Gia said pointedly.

I took a sip of my coffee to collect myself and tried to figure out how to respond to her.

"I can't save you," I said. "Only Jesus can save you." I worried that even that could come across as offensive.

Fortunately, Gia laughed as I went on.

"I thought it would be great to connect over spiritual things, as well as working out," I said. "You and I have been friends for a long time, but we rarely talk about spiritual things. Why not strengthen ourselves spiritually in addition to physically? There isn't any pressure, but I thought I would at least ask."

"Okay, we can try it a couple of times," Gia said tentatively, "but I'm not promising you anything and I don't want you to try and convert me."

Now I laughed and said, "It's up to you how you respond to Jesus. I'm just here to help us explore his teachings together."

Gia and I explored Scripture together twice after our yoga meetings. At times she got defensive and went off about how much Christians had hurt her or how the Bible was full of errors. I tried to stay calm and not get defensive myself, praying silently for the Holy Spirit to open her heart and give me courage and patience. I spent a lot of time praying with my husband after those meetings because I was scared that I was doing more to turn Gia off to Jesus than serving her. My husband's prayers and friendship helped me keep going even when I wanted to quit. He helped me persevere in witness; he knew I needed his help and encouragement to follow Jesus into witness. He was my witness buddy.

Though studying Scripture with Gia was a time filled with both excitement and anxiety for me, I realized that the most important thing I could do was keep pointing her toward Jesus in Scripture and pray for her. I didn't need to defend Christianity. I didn't need to prove the infallibility of Scripture. I didn't need to logically argue about highly political issues and how Christianity had used them to oppress others. I just needed to fix my eyes on Jesus and encourage Gia to do the same thing.

Since that time of basement yoga and breakfast Bible exploration, Gia and I have both moved to new cities and only keep in touch occasionally over Facebook. I don't know what Gia's spiritual life is like currently, but I still pray for her. I can't save her, and I'm not even in close enough proximity anymore to study Scripture with her in person. Though I could have felt like a failure, Jesus and my husband reminded me that I did what I could and was obedient to what Jesus was calling me to do at the time. That is all I could do.

I couldn't save Gia. But I did help her get a glimpse of who Jesus is and how he wants to be present in her life. I did love her and serve her in the small ways I could—offering to pray, bringing a meal, stopping by to talk with her when she was stuck at home with a sick child.

She Did What She Could

I always felt like I could have done more in my relationship with Gia and with many, many other people. And there always is more we could do. But Jesus isn't looking for us to do more; he's asking us to listen to him for what he wants us to do right now to love him and love others. Luke 7:36-38 says,

> When one of the Pharisees invited Jesus to have dinner with him, he went to the Pharisee's house and reclined at the table. A woman in that town who lived a sinful life learned that Jesus was eating at the Pharisee's house, so she came there with an alabaster jar of perfume. As she stood behind him at his feet weeping, she began to wet his feet with her tears. Then she wiped them with her hair, kissed them and poured perfume on them.

The dinner guests are angry with Jesus, both because of the intimate indignity of this sinful woman's washing and anointing his feet with oil, and because the money from the costly perfume could be sold and used to care for the poor. Yet Jesus rebukes them, a bold move for someone who is the guest and supremely insulting to his host.

Then he turned toward the woman and said to Simon, "Do you see this woman? I came into your house. You did not give me any water for my feet, but she wet my feet with her tears and wiped them with her hair. You did not give me a kiss, but this woman, from the time I entered, has not stopped kissing my feet. You did not put oil on my head, but she has poured perfume on my feet. Therefore, I tell you, her many sins have been forgiven—as her great love has shown. But whoever has been forgiven little loves little."

Then Jesus said to her, "Your sins are forgiven." (Luke 7:44-48)

Not only does Jesus rebuke his disciples for scoffing at a woman for wasting a valuable resource, but he also says that wherever the gospel is preached all over the world, her act of love and submission will be remembered (Mark 14:9). Did you catch that? She will be remembered because she poured perfume on Jesus' feet. She used what she had to pour out love to Jesus. We do the same when we offer what we have to love and serve others because of Jesus. Mother Teresa once said, "I have found the paradox, that if you love until it hurts, there can be no more hurt, only more love."

Callused Feet, Tender Hearts

We run the race by, for and through Jesus. It's essential to keep focused on him to remind us that it really is worth it to endure pain, awkwardness and frustration. There are people I've been praying for over the past decade, including my brother, Matt. Though Matt was zealous for Jesus in his youth—rigorously memorizing Scripture and taking risks to participate in overseas mission trips—he began to drift away from Jesus in college. Matt and I lived together in a run-down, mouse-infested duplex for two years after I graduated from college and he had graduated from high school. I can remember making pancakes one Saturday morning and getting

into an apologetic conversation with him about the goodness of
God in spite of the suffering and evil in the world. At the time I
thought it was cool that my brother and I could have such deep
conversations over pancakes, but when it dawned on me that it
wasn't simply an intellectual conversation but a battle going on in
his soul, I was ashamed at how I had responded with such little
compassion, just wanting to seem like a smart Christian.

Over the years Matt and I have had significant conversations
about spiritual things. He's a smart guy—he can speak and read
Arabic and has his PhD in Middle Eastern studies from the University of Connecticut. He's married to Alise, a wonderful Jewish
woman, and they try to make a difference in the world through
helping students learn about the political struggles in the Middle
East and living as devout vegans out of their concern for animal
welfare. I remember being home one Thanksgiving and driving to
get some groceries with Matt. I asked him how things had been
for him spiritually, and he sighed and said, "All right." Not exactly
an open invitation to share the gospel. But as we talked, Matt saw
that I didn't have an agenda in our conversation; I really did want
to know how he was doing spiritually and was open to hear his
questions and doubts.

"I just don't get grace," he shared. "Islam I can understand. You
do the work and God is pleased with you; you go to Mecca and pray
five times a day. Not that I would convert to Islam, but it's this issue
of not needing to do anything for God that is so crazy to me about
Christianity." I agreed with Matt—it *is* crazy that we don't have to
do anything for God to love us or to get his attention. It goes against
everything we're taught about what it means to be successful in life.

As Matt and I talked, he gently asked, "Do you feel like a failure
as an evangelist because you can't save your own brother?"

My eyes widened, amazed he asked such a pointed question. "Matt,
I think the love of Jesus is the best thing out there. But I can't save

you. That's something you have to choose for yourself. I'm not going to hide who I am or the work I do. You know I'm crazy about Jesus."

He laughed and smiled as he turned toward home. "Yeah," he said, "I just don't want you to think it's your fault or something."

Now I laughed. "I know I'm a pretty big screwup and I made you drink a margarita years ago that you spit out and said tasted like poison, but I love you. And God loves you. And I pray that in some small way I can show that to you and keep our conversation open and not get weird about talking about spiritual things."

Matt and I don't talk about spiritual things on a regular basis, but when we do he knows I'm not going to push him into something, that I respect him and want to listen to what he has to say. We're able to continue the conversation because we have mutual respect and love for one another.

My mom and dad and sister and I pray for Matt and his wife regularly. We are waiting and longing for the day that they realize the love of Jesus and that they don't have to do anything to earn his favor, don't have to vote in a certain way to be a Christian, and don't have to give up being a vegan to follow Jesus. He loves them, just as they are. I don't have a "success story" of Matt and his wife becoming Christians; all I have is the story of perseverance, prayer and trusting Jesus that the story isn't finished. And I can love them with the freedom of knowing that Jesus is the one who changes hearts, and serve them with the hope that they will experience the love of Jesus through me and the other people in their lives who follow Jesus.

Go to the places that will help you fix your eyes on Jesus and find comfort and encouragement in the painful and awkward times. Develop a community of women who will help you keep going when you feel discouraged, stupid or afraid. While our feet become calloused from doing activities we love, Jesus is the one who keeps our hearts tender. He is the one who helps calluses develop in the right places. Instead of our hearts growing hard and crusty, Jesus reminds us that we live in a broken world that rejected his love. Listen to worship music, spend time in Scripture or call a friend to ask for prayer as ways of coming back to Jesus instead of licking your wounds and then giving up altogether. The race is too important to drop out.

We look to Jesus to keep running the race each day for the joy set before us. On the other side of pain and nervousness is the joy of surrendering to Jesus, the thrill of seeing friends opening up to his love, and the hope that they will choose to follow him as Savior and Lord. Get out there with your girlfriends and develop some calloused feet and tender hearts together. Jesus has so much goodness for you as you experience and share his love with others.

Response

What is something that you have done that was awkward at first but later became enjoyable? Where was an area of following Jesus that began as uncomfortable but now is a normal and natural part of your life?

Who are people or places you've been tempted to give up on because sharing Jesus has been painful, uncomfortable or awkward? Pray for Jesus to give you the boldness, love and humility to continue to love and serve where he has sent you.

Epilogue

You have a story to tell—the story of Jesus and his love unfolding in your life and community. My prayer for you is that the love of Christ would fill you, the boldness of the Holy Spirit would empower you, and the guidance of God the Father would send you to the people and places that need him. You are part of the great cloud of sisters carrying the message of Jesus wherever you go.

I pray that Jesus would bless your beautiful feet. May the Holy Spirit strengthen them wherever you go and to whomever he sends you. I pray that together we will leave footprints and trails of his love for many more to begin to follow him all across this world. How beautiful are *your* feet that bring good news!

Acknowledgments

This book has been a culmination of joy, soul-searching, sorting through my experiences and listening to the experiences of other women who are seeking to share Jesus. I've been deeply affected by their stories of boldness, the pain they have gone through in following Jesus and the unwavering love of Jesus that drives them forward in mission.

I'm grateful for my community in helping me to pursue this dream. Thanks to my husband, Dave, who helps me to live into who God made me to be—and who knows when I need to chill out and just laugh and watch some SNL. You encourage me to not hold back. I love you. To my sons, Reuben and Oswald—thank you for being patient with a mentally checked-out mommy while I was writing portions of this book. (I'd also like to thank the creators of television shows Ninjago, Word Girl and Bubble Guppies that entertained my sons when I tried to wake up early to write without disturbing them and did so unsuccessfully.) I love you boys. You are my greatest treasures.

My gang—Una Lucey-Lee, Leslie Mulder, Susie Vandergriend and Jessica Thorne. You gals saw me through some really rough stuff while I was writing this book. Thanks for praying for me, taking me out for emergency ice cream and having Skype calls to remind me to be strong and courageous. I cannot underscore your support in this process enough.

Thanks to my family—Cindy, Rich, Rachel, Matthew, Matt, Alise, Joe, Kim, Charles, Gary, Mae Ellen and Rachel for loving me, showing me how to more fully love Jesus, and for cooking and enjoying elaborate, joyful feasts together. I love being at the table with all of you.

To the men and women who have poured into me to help me grow as an evangelist over the years—thank you for your investment. Andrea Thomas, you took a risk hiring me all those years ago even when you had to send back my application three times. R. York Moore, thanks for creating the original regional evangelism team where Dan Geogerian, Dave Biskie, Jesse Roselius and I got to dream big and have some amazing adventures together in sharing Jesus. I treasure the memories of that team, even when you made us listen to Metallica on the road trips. Dr. Rick Richardson, I'm grateful for your mentorship and friendship. You have prayed for me and supported me in my journey for a long time. You will always be "Slick Rick" for your prowess in relating to people in the academy and on the playa. Thanks to Velocity Church Cleveland and Scott Pugh for living out the gospel in a beautiful and compelling way as you love the kids in our city. Much love to Velocity MOPS for being a crew of women trying to be authentic, love Jesus and love your families well.

To the authors who helped me figure out how to write a book—Adam and Christine Jeske, Scott Bessenecker, and Lorilee Craker and Alexandra Kuykendall. Without your practical help, feedback and prophetic words, this book would have never happened. I owe you all cookies. To my editor, Al Hsu—I never understood why people were so grateful to their editors when they wrote a book. Now I understand. You were always in my corner even when this started as a weird little book. You fought for this project to happen. Thanks for helping me persevere.

Jesus, you are my beloved Lord. I would follow you anywhere, sit joyfully at your feet, laugh and play and delight in all your goodness, and suffer for your gospel. You reach out to me with love, even when I am so unloveable. You are my song in the night.

"This is my Father's world: He shines in all that's fair; in the rustling grass I hear him pass; he speaks to me everywhere.

"This is my Father's world. O let me ne'er forget, that though the wrong seems oft so strong, God is the ruler yet.

"This is my Father's world: the battle is not done: Jesus who died shall be satisfied, and earth and heav'n be one."

The Big Story

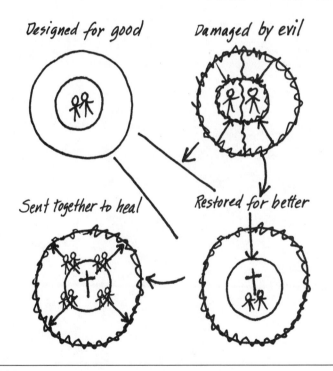

Figure A.1

Becoming comfortable with a gospel outline is essential to evangelism. I've found that the Big Story outline is a great way to connect with

people and share my own story. You can download the Big Story app
for free for iPhone or Android. This app includes an interactive diagram you can share with friends and a way to email it to them as
well as a tutorial of how to use it. Visit the InterVarsity website for
more information about the app (http://evangelism.intervarsity.org/
how/gospel-outline/get-big-story-app), to watch a tutorial video
(http://evangelism.intervarsity.org/how/gospel-outline/big-story
-tutorial-video) and to find out how you can share your story within
the framework of the Big Story (http://evangelism.intervarsity.org/
how/gospel-outline/how-your-story-fits-big-story-outline).

Discussion Guide

Great questions to begin any discussion:

- What resonated with you in this chapter? Are there any Scripture passages that stuck out to you or stories you could relate to?

- What did you disagree with, find confusing or have more questions about?

- What have these dynamics looked like in your own life?

- How does what you're reading influence how you view God, yourself and others?

Chapter 1: Uncomfortable

1. Describe a time when you felt out of place because you were a woman. What questions did it raise in your mind? What doubts did it spark? How did it affect your interactions with other women and men?

2. What are areas in your church or Christian community where you've seen healthy gender relationships modeled? Where are some areas of brokenness and pain you need to confess and pray through?

3. What are ways you can be an advocate for women and girls in your church or community? Consider volunteering others for opportunities that they would be too scared or self-conscious to ask for themselves. Create a program or group to help women and girls develop more confidence in witness. Dream big and pray big!

Chapter 2: We Saw Your Boobs

1. Share a time when you felt like you stuck out from others.

2. Have you ever had a time when you were trying to talk to a guy about Jesus and it was clear he was flirting with you? Describe what that was like.

3. Describe a time when you were ashamed of your body—it could be because of your size, shape, ethnicity, family background or what you were wearing.

Chapter 3: Fashionistas for Jesus

1. Talk about a time when you connected with other women over clothing, shoes, makeup, hair or other things that have been considered "trivial."

2. What strikes you about Tabitha's story? How does it challenge your perspective on clothing and serving others?

3. Where do you interact with people that are in spiritual or physical poverty in your community? What is one way you can pray for them or serve them?

Chapter 4: First-Date Awkwardness

1. Tell a story about an awkward first date that you've had. If you've never been on a date, talk about a time when you wanted to go on a date or strike up a friendship but were too nervous to do so.

2. How do you relate to blogger Anna Gissing's story? Are you hesitant to scatter seed for fear of wasting it? When have you taken a risk to share or demonstrate Jesus and seen some growth happen?

3. Make a list together about what the next appropriate risk might be with a friend who is far from God. It could be anything from initiating a spiritual conversation, taking time to develop a friendship with someone, serving them in a practical way, inviting them to church or beginning to do an investigative Bible discussion with them.

Chapter 5: Choose the Right Shoes

1. Describe the favorite pair of shoes you've ever owned (or wanted to own!).

2. Talk about a time when you felt confident. It doesn't necessarily have to be about evangelism—just think about what helped you to feel confident in that particular situation. How might God want to use that confidence to carry over into witness to others?

3. When have you taken a risk in sharing Jesus with someone? How did you feel? What happened in your relationship with God and with the person as a result?

Chapter 6: Burning Man and the Resurrected Man

1. What is the craziest thing you've ever done for Jesus? It doesn't have to be as crazy as Burning Man—just something that felt fun and risky to you.

2. Take a piece of paper and write down some fears you have about certain groups of people. Take a minute to pray and confess your fears and ask Jesus to open your heart to loving people different from you. Put your papers together and burn

them up in a safe place as a fragrant offering to Jesus demonstrating your trust that he can use you to reach others.

3. Talk with your group about one way you're going to reach out to a community or person that makes you feel nervous. It doesn't need to be anything huge—it could simply be striking up a conversation or beginning to pray for this person or community.

Chapter 7: Connecting God's Story, My Story & Her Story

1. Is there a story you remember from a sermon you've heard or devotional you've read?

2. Write down three ways that Jesus is influencing your life currently. It could be helping you to develop more patience. It could be the realization that you're annoyed with Jesus and don't want to spend time with him.

3. What are some connection points in your own story with the story of someone you know who isn't a Christian?

4. Do you struggle more with listening to others or being vulnerable about your own life?

Chapter 8: Experiments in Loving Others

1. Talk about a time when you demonstrated God's love to someone in a practical way. What did you do? How did you feel before, during and after?

2. Where do you struggle in comparing yourself to other women and how they're living out their faith?

3. How do you determine the way in which Jesus is calling you to follow him? Are there ways that particularly speak to you when you're seeking direction about how Jesus wants you to serve him and share him with others?

Chapter 9: Are You a Peacock or a Pigeon?

1. Talk about a time when you were going through the motions spiritually. What did you do? How did it feel in contrast to a time when you weren't going through the motions? What was different about those times?

2. What are some questions that you have about God or your spiritual life?

3. Share about a time you were afraid to be different and stick out. What fears held you back?

4. Share about a time you felt confident in being yourself. What helped you to feel this way? What are ways you can encourage each other in killing the pigeon and living into the peacock of who God has made you to be?

Chapter 10: Rest and Other Strange Concepts

1. Talk about one thing you like about your body and are grateful for. What's the soundtrack that plays through your mind about yourself or your body? How do you think God feels about that soundtrack? What changes do you think he'd make to what plays through your mind?

2. What do you find yourself escaping into when you're tired, stressed or angry?

3. Share about a time when God helped you to understand something spiritual by using the physical.

4. Treat yo' self! Plan a date with yourself to take a nap, go for a walk or do something else that helps you to rest and enjoy life. Have a girlfriend ask you how your date with yourself was and do the same for her!

Chapter 11: Life Changes, God Is Unchanging

1. Talk about a time in your life when you were really passionate about Jesus. What helped you cultivate and sustain this passion?

2. Is there a woman who has inspired you to live out your faith? What about her life inspires you?

3. Where are you tempted to feed yourself instead of care for the lost sheep? What about this has made it difficult to relate to or build relationships with people far from God?

Chapter 12: Compassionate Calluses

1. What is an area of life that you feel nervous or dread engaging in? What helps you overcome those hurdles and engage in this area of life? Did it eventually become enjoyable?

2. Who could be a witness buddy in your life? What are ways you can encourage each other to run the race with perseverance in reaching people who are far from God?

3. What is one small step of love you can demonstrate to someone whom you have given up on? Perhaps it's praying for them or serving them in a practical way. Is there a group of people that your community tends to neglect or give up on? What is one way you can demonstrate love to this group of people?

Notes

Chapter 1: Uncomfortable

[1]Charming Charlie is a jewelry, clothing and accessory store that sells low cost, sparkly items and has them organized by color. A salt lick is a block of salt used by hunters to attract deer.

[2]Sharon Hodde Miller, "The Seminary Gender Gap," Her.meneutics, *Christianity Today*, May 23, 2013, http://www.christianitytoday.com/women/2013/may/seminary-gender-gap.html.

[3]Ibid.

[4]Carolyn Custis James, *Half the Church* (Grand Rapids: Zondervan, 2011), p. 185.

[5]This frustration mostly arose from evangelism conferences I was attending where the male speakers would lead a time of prayer for the women and children back home. Evangelism conferences often have felt like old boys clubs. It was clear that I was in a minority and not acknowledged.

[6]"Gender-Based Violence," Half the Sky Movement, accessed January 14, 2015, http://www.halftheskymovement.org/issues/gender-based-violence.

Chapter 2: We Saw Your Boobs

"We Saw Your Boobs" was sung by Seth McFarlane at the 2013 Oscars. The song detailed movies in which academy award nominated actresses disrobed. There is always truth in jest and the song made me sad to see these talented women reduced to the sum of their body parts. I also felt like this song could be sung in some churches where women are similarly objectified.

[1]Rachel Pietka, "Hey John Piper, Is My Femininity Showing?," Her.meneutics, *Christianity Today*, April 26, 2013, http://www.christianitytoday.com/women/2013/april/hey-john-piper-is-my-femininity-showing.html.

[2]Ann Boyd, "Flee from Sin," *The Well*, May 28, 2013, http://thewell.intervarsity.org/blog/flee-sin.

[3]*Yellow fever* is a slang term for men who fetishize or show a strong preference for Asian women.

[4]"What (Not) to Wear: A Female Pastor Prepares to Preach (Part 1)," Leadership

Journal, *Christianity Today*, January 20, 2014, http://www.christianitytoday.com /parse/2014/january/what-not-to-wear.html. I found it indicative of how divisive and painful the issue is that the author chose to remain anonymous.

[5]Brenda Salter McNeil, *A Credible Witness: Reflections on Power, Evangelism and Race* (Downers Grove, IL: InterVarsity Press, 2008).

[6]For all you youngsters who have no idea what 555-1212 is, it's the number we used to dial on a telephone for information—to check the weather or other things before we had the Google machine.

[7]Nikki A. Toyama and Tracey Gee, eds., *More Than Serving Tea* (Downers Grove, IL: InterVarsity Press, 2006), p. 164.

[8]Ibid., p. 165.

Chapter 3: Fashionistas for Jesus

[1]Lynne Hybels, "My Sister's Keeper," Lynne Hybel's personal website, accessed January 21, 2015, http://www.lynnehybels.com/my-sisters-keeper/.

[2]Rachel's stories about her ministry at makeup counters could fill an entire book. I need to mine her brain for more stories like these.

[3]Yes, I realize there is the word *bitch* in this book. You will also find the words *piss* and *damned* if you choose to keep reading this book. If this is offensive, please take a deep breath, try to see the forest instead of just an offensive tree and think about the relationships that these women who didn't know Jesus were building with Deb and the other ladies.

[4]Alan Hirsch and Debra Hirsch, *Untamed: Reactivating a Missional Form of Discipleship* (Grand Rapids: Baker Books, 2010), p. 148.

Chapter 4: First-Date Awkwardness

[1]I am still convinced that there are probably sharks in the Great Lakes. At the Cleveland Museum of Natural History there is a skeleton of a giant prehistoric shark called Dunkleosteus. I know some sort of creepy shark relative is probably lurking in the cold waters of Lake Superior somewhere. If you happen to be a shark researcher and can confirm this fact, don't tell me. I want to live under the illusion that the Great Lakes are shark-free.

[2]Anna Moseley Gissing, "What Does It Feel Like to Be the Farmer?," *The Well*, October 14, 2014, http://thewell.intervarsity.org/reflections/what-does-it -feel-be-farmer.

Chapter 5: Choose the Right Shoes

[1]For more on the demise of Zima, check out Slate.com's article "The Long, Slow, Torturous Death of Zima," www.slate.com/articles/life/drink/2008/11/the_long_slow_torturous_death_of_zima.html.

[2]"Prayer of Examen," http://www.seattlevineyard.org/files/prayer_of_examen.pdf. For a modern adaptation of the Spiritual Exercises, see Larry Warner, *Journey with Jesus: Discovering the Spiritual Exercises of Saint Ignatius* (Downers Grove, IL: InterVarsity Press, 2010).

[3]Having clean socks and underwear for my family every day is amazing. I highly recommend having enough margin in your life for this to happen for you too.

[4]Alan J. Roxburgh and M. Scott Boren, *Introducing the Missional Church* (Grand Rapids: Baker, 2009), p. 87.

[5]I don't think I've ever used the word "bullhonkey" but for some reason that's the one that came to mind.

Chapter 6: Burning Man and the Resurrected Man

[1]Alan Taylor, "Burning Man 2014," *The Atlantic*, September 1, 2014, http://www.theatlantic.com/infocus/2014/09/burning-man-2014/100802/.

[2]"The 10 Principles of Burning Man," Burning Man, accessed January 30, 2015, http://burningman.org/culture/philosophical-center/10-principles.

[3]Jessica Fick, "The Omission Trip," Jessica Fick personal website, August 17, 2010, http://jessicaleepfick.com/2010/08/the-omission-trip/.

[4]If you're reading this chapter and thinking to yourself, "Cool . . . I totally want to go to Burning Man!" you should know that going there can be a disarming, disturbing experience. For many people, including myself and other members of our team, it brought out deep insecurities, fears and other areas of brokenness. Just remember to prayerfully ask Jesus, "Lord, is this something you're inviting me to do? Or do I want to do this just to feel like a cool Christian?"

[5]I am especially struck by Philip's story in the context of today's worship of superpastors of megachurches. I love Philip's radical demonstration of dying to self when it is confusing, seems bizarre and is so out of his control.

[6]Sergew Hable Selassie, *The Church of Ethiopia: A Panorama of History and Spiritual Life* (Addis Ababa: Ethiopian Orthodox Church, 1970), excerpted at http://www.ethiopianorthodox.org/english/ethiopian/prechristian.html.

Chapter 7: Connecting God's Story, My Story & Her Story

[1]Rick Richardson, *Reimagining Evangelism: Inviting Friends on a Spiritual Journey* (Downers Grove, IL: InterVarsity Press, 2006), pp. 84-87.

[2]Christine Dillon, *Telling the Gospel Through Story: Evangelism That Keeps Hearers Wanting More* (Downers Grove, IL: InterVarsity Press, 2012), p. 28.

[3]James Choung, *True Story: A Christianity Worth Believing In* (Downers Grove, IL: InterVarsity Press, 2008).

[4]Beau Crosetto, *Beyond Awkward: When Talking About Jesus Is Outside Your Comfort Zone* (Downers Grove, IL: InterVarsity Press, 2014), p. 203.

[5]John Gerzema and Michael D'Antonio, *The Athena Doctrine: How Women (and the Men Who Think Like Them) Will Rule the Future* (San Francisco: Jossey-Bass, 2013), p. 260.

[6]Ibid., p. 263.

[7]Catherine Clark Kroeger and Mary J. Evans, eds., *The IVP Women's Bible Commentary* (Downers Grove, IL: InterVarsity Press, 2002), p. 574.

[8]Prathia L. Hall, "Encounters with Jesus from Dying to Life: Mark 5:21-43," in *Power in the Pulpit*, ed. Cleophus J. LaRue (Louisville, KY: Westminster John Knox, 2002), pp. 68-69. Prathia Hall's essay is worth reading. She gracefully honors women and men by preaching this text to a mixed audience on Father's Day. You can learn more about her and other amazing African American women preachers at theafricanamericanlectionary.org.

[9]Philip Jenkins, *The New Faces of Christianity: Believing the Bible in the Global South* (New York: Oxford University Press, 2006), p. 169.

[10]Ibid., p. 171.

[11]Jessica Fick, "Why the Gospel Is Good News for You," Spring Arbor University, Morning Chapel, Spring Arbor, Michigan, September 22, 2014, http://sites.arbor.edu/livestream/2014/10/16/chapel-september-22-2014 -jessica-fick.

Chapter 8: Experiments in Loving Others

[1]My husband and friends are generous and patient with me when I have come up with a new idea I'm excited about. And often, they help me work to make it a reality.

[2]I've seen many friends walk through amazing and heartbreaking stories of adoption and foster care. I'm amazed by the love and grace of each of these families that love profoundly (I'm talking to you, Eerdmans, Carlisles and

Douds). Jacki and Patrick's story was unfolding as I was writing this book and was the freshest in my mind.

[3]Alan Hirsch and Dave Ferguson, *On the Verge: A Journey into the Apostolic Future of the Church* (Grand Rapids: Zondervan, 2011), p. 125.

[4]John G. Stackhouse Jr., *Evangelical Landscapes: Facing Critical Issues of the Day* (Grand Rapids: Baker Academic, 2002), p. 22.

[5]Nadia Bolz-Weber, *Pastrix: The Cranky, Beautiful Faith of a Sinner & Saint* (New York: Jericho Books, 2013).

[6]Sally Lloyd-Jones, *The Jesus Storybook Bible* (Grand Rapids: Zondervan, 2007), p. 36.

Chapter 9: Are You a Peacock or a Pigeon?

[1]The Rockefeller Greenhouse is a small gem of Cleveland. It's worth a visit and is free if you're able to go. On a nice day you can also stroll the cultural gardens and enjoy the fountains and sculptures from different countries.

[2]I have always had a vivid imagination. Encountering God in this way was like someone tore the roof off of my mind and invited me to sail free with the Holy Spirit.

[3]Gary Neal Hansen, *Kneeling with Giants: Learning to Pray with History's Best Teachers* (Downers Grove, IL: InterVarsity Press, 2012), pp. 107-8.

Chapter 10: Rest and Other Strange Concepts

[1]James Bryan Smith, *The Good and Beautiful God: Falling in Love with the God Jesus Knows* (Downers Grove, IL: InterVarsity Press, 2009), p. 34.

[2]Arlie Hochschild and Anne Machung, *The Second Shift: Working Families and the Revolution at Home* (New York: Penguin, 2003), quoted in Sarah A. Burgard, Jennifer A. Ailshire and N. Michelle Hughes, "Gender and Sleep Duration Among American Adults" (Population Studies Center, University of Michigan Institute for Social Research, special report, June 2010), http://www.psc.isr.umich.edu/pubs/pdf/rr09-693.pdf.

[3]While working on this book I learned that I have hypothyroidism—a disorder of the autoimmune system that causes unexplained weight gain and severe fatigue. This struggle of being too tired to do anything has been very real to me whether because of depression or because of having low thyroid. If you've been struggling to make it through the day without a nap, it's worth getting your thyroid checked out since it's a very common problem among women.

[4]"Depression in Women: Understanding the Gender Gap," Mayo Clinic, January 19, 2013, http://www.mayoclinic.org/diseases-conditions/depression /in-depth/depression/art-20047725.

[5]Ibid.

[6]Ruth Haley Barton, *Invitation to Solitude and Silence: Experiencing God's Transforming Presence* (Downers Grove, IL: InterVarsity Press, 2004), pp. 58-59.

[7]Ibid., p. 60.

[8]Dallas Willard, *The Great Omission: Reclaiming Jesus's Essential Teachings on Discipleship* (San Francisco: HarperSanFrancisco, 2006), p. 89.

[9]I'm learning to lay down in green pastures through self-care. I'm prone to emotional eating, so I've been experimenting with other ways to feel refreshed. Taking a twenty minute break to read some poetry, embroider, drink a cup of tea out of a pretty teacup, take a short walk, light a candle or schedule lunch with a friend have all been ways that have helped me to slow down and not push myself so hard every day.

[10]Kirsten Weir, "The Exercise Effect," *American Psychological Association* 42, no. 11 (December 2011): 48, http://www.apa.org/monitor/2011/12/exercise .aspx.

[11]Rachel Marie Stone, *Eat with Joy: Redeeming God's Gift of Food* (Downers Grove, IL: InterVarsity Press, 2013), pp. 100-101.

[12]Charles H. Spurgeon, "Psalm 23," *The Treasury of David*, The Spurgeon Archive, accessed February 4, 2015, http://www.spurgeon.org/treasury /ps023.htm.

Chapter 11: Life Changes, God Is Unchanging

[1]Timothy Keller, *Counterfeit Gods: The Empty Promises of Money, Sex, and Power, and the Only Hope That Matters* (New York: Dutton, 2009), p. 146.

[2]"Hildegard of Bingen," *Wikipedia*, last modified February 2, 2015, http://en .wikipedia.org/wiki/Hildegard_of_Bingen.

[3]PBS.org, "Religious Experience and Journal of Mrs. Jarena Lee," Africans in America, Part 3 (1791–1831), www.pbs.org/wgbh/aia/part3/3h1638.html.

[4]Aimee Semple McPherson's story is incredible, inspiring and heartbreaking. For a fascinating biography of her life check out Daniel Mark Epstein's book *Sister Aimee: The Life of Aimee Semple McPherson*. If you happen to be near Silver Lake in LA you can actually visit her home. It's been turned into a museum and church that continues to have a thriving ministry.

[5]Kate Harris, *Wonder Women: Navigating the Challenges of Motherhood, Career, and Identity* (Grand Rapids: Zondervan, 2013), p. 26.

Chapter 12: Compassionate Calluses

[1]Katty Kay and Claire Shipman, *The Confidence Code: The Science and Art of Self-Assurance—What Women Should Know* (New York: HarperCollins, 2014), chap. 6. *The Confidence Code* is a profound book exploring how women cultivate confidence. There is even an online test you can take to help you figure out how to grow your confidence: http://theconfidencecode.com/confidence-quiz.

Bibliography

Anonymous. "What (Not) to Wear: A Female Pastor Prepares to Preach (Part 1)." *PARSE. Leadership Journal*, January 20, 2014. http://www.christianitytoday.com/parse/2014/january/what-not-to-wear.html.

Barton, Ruth Haley. *Invitation to Solitude and Silence: Experiencing God's Transforming Presence*. Downers Grove, IL: InterVarsity Press, 2004.

Bolz-Weber, Nadia. *Pastrix: The Cranky, Beautiful Faith of a Sinner & Saint*. New York: Jericho, 2013.

Burgard, Sarah A., Jennifer A. Ailshire and Michelle N. Hughes. "Gender and Sleep Duration Among American Adults." *Population Studies Center Research Report 09-693*. Population Studies Center, revised June 2010. http://www.psc.isr.umich.edu/pubs/pdf/rr09-693.pdf.

Choung, James. *True Story*. Downers Grove, IL: InterVarsity Press, 2008.

Crosetto, Beau. *Beyond Awkward: When Talking About Jesus Is Outside Your Comfort Zone*. Downers Grove, IL: InterVarsity Press, 2014.

"Depression in Women: Understanding the Gender Gap." Mayo Clinic, January 19, 2013. www.mayoclinic.org/diseases-conditions/depression/in-depth/depression/art-20047725.

DeRusha, Michelle. *50 Women Every Christian Should Know: Learning from Heroines of the Faith*. Grand Rapids: Baker, 2014.

Dillon, Christine. *Telling the Gospel Through Story: Evangelism That Keeps Hearers Wanting More*. Downers Grove, IL: InterVarsity Press, 2012.

Foster, Richard J. *Celebration of Discipline: The Path to Spiritual Growth*. San Francisco: Harper & Row, 1988.

Gissing, Anna M. "What Does It Feel Like to Be the Farmer?" *The Well*, October 14, 2014. http://thewell.intervarsity.org/reflections/what-does-it-feel-be-farmer.

Hall, Prathia L. "Encounters with Jesus from Dying to Life: Mark 5:21-43." In *Power in the Pulpit: How America's Most Effective Black Preachers Prepare Their Sermons*, edited by Cleophus J. LaRue. Louisville, KY: Westminster John Knox, 2002.

Hansen, Gary Neal. *Kneeling with Giants: Learning to Pray with History's Best Teachers*. Downers Grove, IL: InterVarsity Press, 2012.

Harris, Kate. *Wonder Women: Navigating the Challenges of Motherhood, Career, and Identity*. Grand Rapids: Zondervan, 2013.

Hirsch, Alan, and Dave Ferguson. *On the Verge: A Journey into the Apostolic Future of the Church*. Grand Rapids: Zondervan, 2011.

Hirsch, Alan, and Debra Hirsch. *Untamed: Reactivating a Missional Form of Discipleship*. Grand Rapids: Baker, 2010.

Hochschild, Arlie Russell, and Anne Machung. *The Second Shift*. New York: Penguin, 2003.

Hodde Miller, Sharon. "The Seminary Gender Gap." *Christianity Today*, May 23, 2013. http://www.christianitytoday.com/women/2013/may/seminary-gender-gap.html.

Hybels, Lynne. "My Sister's Keeper." *Lynne Hybels*. www.lynnehybels.com/my-sisters-keeper.

James, Carolyn Custis. *Half the Church: Recapturing God's Global Vision for Women*. Grand Rapids: Zondervan, 2011.

James, Carolyn Custis. *Lost Women of the Bible: Finding Strength and Significance Through Their Stories*. Grand Rapids: Zondervan, 2005.

Jenkins, Philip. *The New Faces of Christianity: Believing the Bible in the Global South*. Oxford: Oxford University Press, 2006.

Kay, Katty, and Claire Shipman. *The Confidence Code: The Science and Art of Self-assurance—What Women Should Know*. New York: HarperCollins, 2014.

Keller, Timothy J. *Counterfeit Gods: The Empty Promises of Money, Sex, and Power, and the Only Hope That Matters*. New York: Dutton, 2009.

Lloyd-Jones, Sally. *The Jesus Storybook Bible: Every Story Whispers His Name*. Grand Rapids: Zondervan, 2007.

McNeil, Brenda Salter. *A Credible Witness: Reflections on Power, Evangelism and Race*. Downers Grove, IL: InterVarsity Press, 2008.

Pietka, Rachel. "Hey John Piper, Is My Femininity Showing?" Her.meneutics. *Christianity Today*, April 26, 2013. http://www.christianitytoday.com /women/2013/april/hey-john-piper-is-my-femininity-showing.html.

Pippert, Rebecca Manley. *Out of the Saltshaker and into the World: Evangelism as a Way of Life*. Downers Grove, IL: InterVarsity Press, 1979.

Roxburgh, Alan J., M. Scott Boren and Mark Priddy. *Introducing the Missional Church: What It Is, Why It Matters, How to Become One*. Grand Rapids: Baker, 2009.

Smith, James Bryan. *The Good and Beautiful God: Falling in Love with the God Jesus Knows*. Downers Grove, IL: InterVarsity Press, 2009.

Spurgeon, C. H. *The Treasury of David*. The Spurgeon Archive. http://www .spurgeon.org/treasury/treasury.htm.

Stackhouse, John G. *Evangelical Landscapes: Facing Critical Issues of the Day*. Grand Rapids: Baker Academic, 2002.

Starbuck, Margot. *Small Things with Great Love: Adventures in Loving Your Neighbor*. Downers Grove, IL: InterVarsity Press, 2011.

Stone, Rachel Marie. *Eat with Joy: Redeeming God's Gift of Food*. Downers Grove, IL: InterVarsity Press, 2013.

Toyama-Szeto, Nikki A., and Tracey Gee, eds. *More Than Serving Tea: Asian American Women on Expectations, Relationships, Leadership and Faith*. Downers Grove, IL: InterVarsity Press, 2006.

Warner, Larry. *Journey with Jesus: Discovering the Spiritual Exercises of Saint Ignatius*. Downers Grove, IL: InterVarsity Press, 2010.

Weir, Kirsten. "The Exercise Effect." *Monitor on Psychology* 42, no. 11. American Psychological Association. www.apa.org/monitor/2011/12 /exercise.aspx.

Willard, Dallas. *The Great Omission: Reclaiming Jesus's Essential Teachings on Discipleship*. San Francisco, CA: HarperSanFrancisco, 2006.

Wright, N. T. *Surprised by Hope: Rethinking Heaven, the Resurrection, and the Mission of the Church*. New York: HarperOne, 2008.

Contact Page

I long to see a global community of women unleashed to share their faith in Jesus. I'd love to hear your stories of success, failure, prayerful perseverance and celebration when you lead people to Christ. Please contact me at jessicafick@gmail.com or on my blog at jessicaleepfick .com to share these stories as an encouragement and testimony of the power of the Holy Spirit moving in you and your community.

Twitter: @JessicaLeepFick
Facebook: EvangelistJessicaLeepFick